Growing Up and ?

in

Two Very Different Cultures

A Journey Through Life
guided by Classical Indian Dance

Cliff Harvey

Growing Up and Thriving in Two Very Different Cultures

Copyright © 2023 Cliff Harvey

All rights reserved.

ISBN: **9798866386024**

DEDICATION

This book is dedicated to the dancers of the Nritham Dance Academy and their extraordinary teacher Sujatha Chenilath who welcomed me so warmly when I asked if I might photograph their progress over a period of several years. Add to this the unconditional love and support given to the students by their parents, many of whom I've become good friends with..

CONTENTS

	Acknowledgments	i
1	Meet the author	Pg 1
2	Introduction	Pg 3
3	About this book	Pg 5
4	Early Days	Pg 9
5	Preparation Days	Pg 27
6	Graduation Days	Pg 83
7	Epilogue	Pg 159

ACKNOWLEDGMENTS

This book would not have been possible without the help and encouragement provided by numerous people.

Mrs. Sujatha Chenilath. As you'll see below, she is the reason I became so interested in documenting the unique dancing I watched at a community event right after I moved to England in 2013. Her dedication to the art is only exceeded by the love and admiration she has for her many hundreds of students. She's the original 'mother hen' to them, blessed with an infinite amount of patience for teaching them the proper, precise way to tell stories through hand gestures, arm and leg movements, eyes, indeed, their entire being. And her students return that love and attention by growing from nervous youngsters, some as young as four years old, into confident and self-assured 16-18 year olds. She is tireless, and I'm sure there's a special place in heaven for her.

The parents. For each student there was always two parents close by, making sure their child was listening to the guru and being treated well. Were it not for Sujatha assuring the parents that she trusted me and they could as well, I would never have gotten past the front door!

The students. At first they were all apprehensive about who I was and what I was doing, but after a month or so of my sitting on the sidelines and watch-ing their practices, and showing them the photographs I'd taken without them knowing I'd done so, they soon warmed to my presence and, finally, what every photographer dreams of being in this sort of project, they more-or-less ignored me; I became nearly invisible to them. I made sure they all had prints to take home to their parents, and I now consider many of them, the students, to be my friends.

Vaughan Dean. I can count on one hand (with fingers left over) the number of people I consider to be best friends, and Vaughan is one of those. We met when he joined the Bedford Camera Club several years ago, and we struck up a friendship almost immediately. He's always been interested in photography, and I did my best to pass on what I knew about the art. But were it not for his complete and total support of me with this project, it would not have been the book it's become. He was the one person who did all the setup work putting this book together and getting it to the stage of production. His help and friendship were paramount with this total effort. Thanks Vaughan, for always being there.

"Only by being part of the story is it possible to tell it."

Irene Trancossi, Photographer

Throughout these pages you will see some of the same faces as they grow back and forth into two very different cultures. You will witness the unconscious transitions the students make between one life and the other, two lives completely different from each other. Because of this learning experience, they will undoubtedly become better, more capable and confident adults. Obtaining that level will be, to a large part, because Mrs. Sujatha Chenilath was in their lives. Her love for, and dedication to, these students is a large part of why their early development into being well prepared human beings will be so successful.

Images by Cliff Harvey and Vaughan Dean

1 MEET THE AUTHOR

Cliff Harvey is a retired firefighter and ex-pat American living in England since 2013. He has been enthusiastic about photography since the early 1960s when, as an Airman with the US Air Force, he was stationed at RAF Chicksands, just outside of Bedford, Bedfordshire. While there, he fell in love with England and all that it represented, so he bought a Pentax Spotmatic camera to record his life there. He's enjoyed meeting and working with people all his adult life, so portrait photography soon became his love. Recall that England (and especially London) was known as the 'Swingin' Sixties' during the time he was here, so there were plenty of opportunities for him to enjoy what had turned into his passion.

Between leaving the USAF in 1966 and retiring from the Boulder, Colorado Fire Department in 1995, he held numerous other positions during his off -duty time, all to do with photography. As well as teaching The Dynamics of Fire at the Fire College in Moreton-on-Marsh in the Cotswolds, he completed hundreds of commissions for modeling brochure work and local fashion shoots, and was the club photographer for the Denver (Colorado, USA) Playboy club for several years as well.

Retirement meant moving to the coast of Oregon USA, where he found copious wildlife, nature and sunsets to record. A change in his family situation meant finding new surroundings, and his love and memories of England came back to him. But regardless, wherever he was, wherever he made a life, his real passion continued - continues - to be people photography.

But he didn't want to just take photographs, he wanted to tell stories with those images. Since he'd already struck up a friendship with a local teacher of classical Indian dancing, the idea of documenting the growth of her young students into not only exceptional dancers, but also outstanding young adults, became the focus which would turn into this book.

2 INTRODUCTION

I'll start by giving the reader a better idea of the people I worked with on this project, the Nritham Dance Academy.

The Nritham Dance Academy is based in Bedford, Bedfordshire, England. They currently have 13 centres around East Anglia and they've been teaching all forms of Indian Classical, Indian Folk and Bollywood dances since 2005. They've been part of major events organized by various Councils like the Bedford River Festival, Kettfest, Northampton Diwali, Cambridge Mela and Stevenage Day, to name just a few. They've also conducted various workshops in and around schools. The Academy is guided and led by its current Artistic Director, Mrs. Sujatha Chenilath, an exponent of the dance forms of Bharatnatyam, Mohiniattam, Kathakali and other folk dances of India. She is also the Director of the Elite Performing Arts Examination Board UK.

The Academy specializes in providing a curriculum in the dance form of Bharatanatyam which is an ancient and classical art form of southern India. The Academy teaches the art form based on techniques, principles and quality of instruction of "Natyashastra" and "Abhinayadarpanam". They also provide a learning platform for other Indian classical dance forms, such as Mohiniattam, Bollywood dance and Indian Classical Music.

3 ABOUT THIS BOOK

Beliefs
One of the many things I've learned from this project about the Nritham Dance Academy is to immerse myself in the community I'm trying to illustrate before I begin my photography. Having said that, although one needs to understand where they are and have respect for the people, this doesn't mean they have to move into the community to photograph it. The point here is that one doesn't have to live a subject's life to make something meaningful. But you do have to know enough to show up and see as deeply and clearly as you can once you're there.

You also have to be clear about why you're there. Why have you decided to document this particular community? How does your subjective viewpoint connect with the actual subject? What is it that you want to say about them? What is it that they might want to say about themselves?! And how can you bring those things together in some way through photography?

I've learned, or come to believe from making photographs with Nritham, that the best work tends to result not from the imposition of an idea on a situation, but from being responsive to what is going on once I get there. Otherwise, what results is merely the illustration of an idea. Don't get me wrong, the idea is still meaningful, because it's the impetus that gets me out the door. But once I get there, the work has to be driven by the experiences I'm actually having, the people I'm actually meeting, and my best attempt at honestly and clearly describing these encounters with my photographs. And then, hopefully, this process leads to something more than what I expected. With the Nritham project, this has usually been the case (luckily..!).

I believe there is an interesting story to every person. The challenge is how to make that visible. Merely pointing the camera at a subject looking into the lens is not going to do it.

As a photographer, you have to have the confidence to not know exactly what you're going to do, but to go forward anyway.

From my experience with Nritham, I discovered that as a photographer, you must find a way to make the camera seemingly disappear, so it's almost transparent. During the moment that I'm photographing, especially for costume/formal images, the space we're in is often a quiet, contemplative space.

Thinking about projects, specifically Nritham, although I enjoy the monochrome application for its textures and tones, colour adds a degree of specificity to the description of a subject that makes the experience of the person more palpable and immediate. So the Nritham project contains both colour and monochrome images.

Lighting
I have always tried to stay away from anything other than natural lighting, from fear and unknowingness (is that even a word?!) with how to use artificial lighting correctly. But I now understand that regardless, once one figures out what lighting works and what backdrop works, once those decisions are made, just start making your images. Take all that other stuff, pack it up and put it away. All those other things are just distractions. From that point on you need to stay focused on what matters; which is the person in front of the lens.

Almost immediately after the idea of a project about Nritham came into my head, I conceptualized the work as something I wanted, *needed!*, to be more broadly accessible. I wanted the 'stories' I was recording to live in an actual, book. That's a much more permanent way of presenting your project and yourself, than being online or in an exhibition!

Reflecting still
As I look back on the Nritham project, there was always this huge, looming potential for failure as I was working on making the images. And I suspect that's something every artist knows or feels. When I'm working, I face a kind of wall, but I also have this idea in front of me and I keep pushing ahead, hoping that it happens. I just knew the Nritham project had to

happen, and I had to do all that I could to make it happen, by simply continuing to work on it!

Lesson learned?
Just make images you believe matter and that have the capacity to transform the viewer, and by extension, the larger social community. Having seen your images, viewers will have the potential to go back out into the world with new information and new perceptions, a transformed world view if you will. This probably sounds like an overly ambitious agenda, but as I see it now, it really is the *only* agenda.

Photographer Bert Stern said "When a portrait evokes a feeling, then you've got something. Technique isn't really important. What I want is a believable moment." Bert Stern is right on.

As photographers, we use stories to shape our experiences into something that will inform and entertain those around us. There is a hunger for stories and a desire to tell them. Stories help us to understand the world and connect with each other.

Why this specific subject?
Our initial research indicated there are approximately 400 Indian and Asian dance studios and academies throughout the United Kingdom, and we believed that all of the students enrolled, as well as the facilities generally, would be most interested in a publication which focuses on what they provide in their area of expertise and influence, and therefore encourage others to look into being a part of that experience. And that would be just those 400 facilities, not to mention other buyers who've not heard of this artistry but would perhaps be interested in learning more about it. There was certainly a need for this book to be done!

But what credentials did I have to tell such a story? Do you remember what photographer Irene Trancossi said?: "Only by being part of the story is it possible to tell it."

After approaching Sujatha with our idea and feeling her enthusiasm, we (Vaughan and I) were invited to start the project by attending a practice session which was also attended by the parents of the young students. I explained to the parents what we had planned, and after they were told that Sujatha had known me for several years and that she trusted me, the enthusiasm spread out over the parents as well.

The photography portion of the project took approximately 18 months to complete. I worked exclusively with the Nritham Dance Academy, primarily from their Kempston location. Sujatha is a very caring and warm individual, and these attributes have not gone unnoticed. She was nominated by the Lord Lieutenant of Northamptonshire (Representative of the King) to attend HM King Charles III Concert on the grounds of Windsor Castle the day after his coronation. This very talented lady has been recognized as one of the people in the UK who do great things with the skills they have, and she was being recognized for having touched and enhanced the lives of literally thousands of young people.

Vaughan and I presented two very successful community exhibitions, one in December of 2022 and another in August of 2023, both of which received a great deal of positive feedback. And since the work was so widely and warmly accepted, I thought we should share our experiences with the general public in the form of a proper book!

The underlying intent of the project, which we're always looking for first and foremost, is emotion. Dance isn't just about movement, it's also about language. As dancers they are learning to speak - tell a story - with their hands, arms, poses; indeed their entire bodies. *That*, is what I try to capture. As dancers they are saying something - telling a story - with their dance movements, and I have them show me what they're trying to say. The end result is to transfer that emotion and dedication from the dancers, to the viewers of the images. If the comments received at the exhibitions are any indication, that goal has been met.

After researching this genre, we found few books available on this specific subject, with most being outdated and, especially in hardback, expensive. This book follows several age groups through their journey learning these historically important dances, while all other publications focus specifically on the movements. This book adds value by showing the journey that the dedicated and enthusiastic young Asians are involved in; their western lives coupled with their cultural upbringing and traditions.

Lastly, I decided to push forward with this book because it's an important story to tell. There is a large Indian and Asian population living in the UK. The culture is founded on family values, respect for others, and a dedication to continuing the art of traditional storytelling. Therefore, a book which celebrates that culture is overdue. I hope you enjoy the fruits of our labour!

4 EARLY DAYS

A Sunday morning. The 10th of October 2021. Vaughan and I visited the location where the Bedford group of the Nritham Dance Academy and guru Sujatha Chenilath would practice each week. Scheduled was a pseudo dress rehearsal, where the students were going to demonstrate for their parents what they had learned so far in their early training. As it turned out, this was a watershed day for us.

The students were prepared when we arrived. They were dressed in costumes of various levels of authenticity, because after all, many of them were pre-teens, and it wasn't unusual for some of them to drop out of the lessons.

The parents were beaming. All the mums and many of the dads were there. Sujatha was in her best finery as she welcomed us all to watch as the students demonstrated the first storytelling dance moves they had learned. But before starting the festivities, she introduced Vaughan and me to the room - especially the parents - and explained who we were - we were outsiders after all - and what we were doing there. But before I explained our proposal, Sujatha said this, roughly in her words.

"I want you all to know that I have known Cliff since about 2014, when he photographed a demonstration of the skills another class of students presented at an outdoor festival held at Priory Country Park. He was kind enough to share his photos with me, and I was taken by what a good job he had done. He did some further photos over the next few years, also shared those with me, and we became friends. So when Cliff approached me with a proposal which he'll tell you about in a minute, I was intrigued and excited. Hopefully we will be seeing Cliff and his colleague Vaughan many times over the coming weeks and months, and I want you all to know that I trust Cliff fully."

With those words, I thanked Sujatha for her kind words, addressed the parents, and introduced our proposal. We wanted to put together a photography project which highlighted the journey being taken by these students - one or two or even three separate classes - as they move between their Indian culture and traditions, and growing up in a British world with British cultures and traditions. We then hoped to not only have a small exhibition of our work which would be open to the public, but also thought about producing a high quality book of some sort that would immortalize the events of what would become the previous two years.

One or both of us were going to attend practice sessions every Sunday morning, observe, and take photographs during the practices. We knew that young students would have a high degree of self-consciousness, so becoming invisible to them, certainly at the start of the project, would be very important. Becoming invisible to the students once they got used to one or the other of us constantly looking at them and taking pictures was the primary goal. And in fact, once I'd been there every Sunday morning for 4-6 weeks in a row, only occasionally seen raising my camera, the students did, in fact, begin to ignore me.

Of course it didn't hurt that I would print some of the keepers from the Sunday previous, bring them along to the next practice session, and show the by then giggling students what they looked like while learning traditional Indian dancing! I allowed - even encouraged - them to keep the photographs and let their parents see them too. With this gesture on our part, the parents received constant reassurance that our project had merits, and they needn't be concerned about what we were doing or how we were doing it.

On the following pages are examples of the many hundreds of images captured during that time; the attention and dedication shown by the students is more than evident. And remember please, each image was simply a moment caught in time; not posed, just selected.

The first few images in this section were captured on the morning we were introduced to the parents and students. Many had arrived in some form of traditional dress, but as you will see as you work your way through this book, the initial photos are just the beginning of our journey. None of the students had been photographed 'professionally' before, so reluctance and apprehension are clearly evident!

Growing Up and Thriving in Two Very Different Cultures

Growing Up and Thriving in Two Very Different Cultures

Growing Up and Thriving in Two Very Different Cultures

Growing Up and Thriving in Two Very Different Cultures

Constant repetition of basic moves instills them in muscle memory.

Growing Up and Thriving in Two Very Different Cultures

Growing Up and Thriving in Two Very Different Cultures

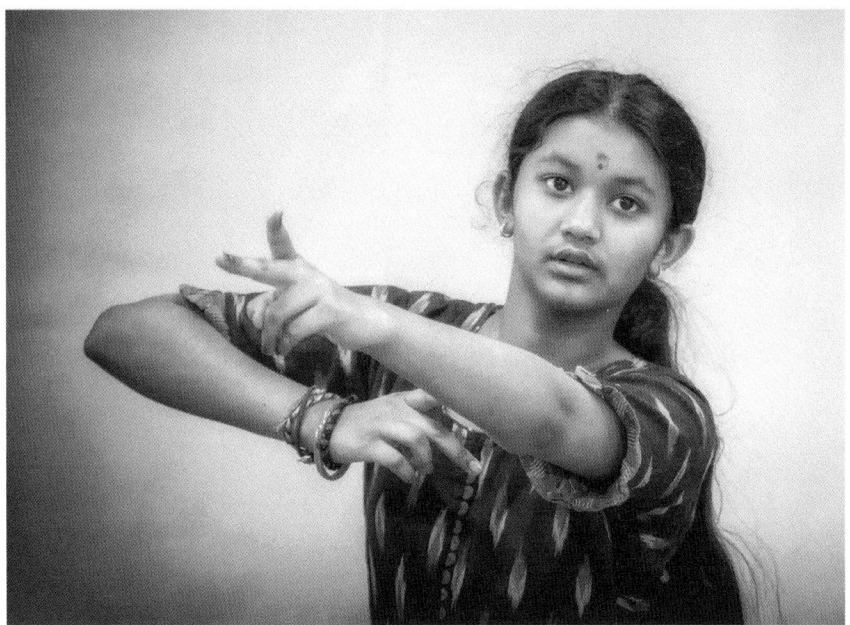

A few months into the project the students were so used to my being there and pointing a camera at them , they'd ceased to be self-conscious and were totally focused on the task in hand; learning the story behind the dance they were doing.

Growing Up and Thriving in Two Very Different Cultures

Growing Up and Thriving in Two Very Different Cultures

Growing Up and Thriving in Two Very Different Cultures

Growing Up and Thriving in Two Very Different Cultures

Growing Up and Thriving in Two Very Different Cultures

Notice the expression on the student's face? Showing the emotion required for that particular part of the story being told.

Growing Up and Thriving in Two Very Different Cultures

Growing Up and Thriving in Two Very Different Cultures

Growing Up and Thriving in Two Very Different Cultures

5 PREPARATION DAYS

These were the days when the students of the Bedford group began to feel comfortable with their routines, actually having developed exact memories - muscle memories if you will - of what moves or motions come after the ones before. These were the days when their comfort began to appear palpable, where their facial expressions and movements had turned from confusion or frustration into confidence and self-assurance. The photos shown in this section will illustrate how comfortable they began to feel, not only good about themselves, but also good about where and how they fit into the process and routines they'd learned.

They begin to work together intuitively. They begin to share with each other things that looked good but were actually improvisations of what they should have done. And even at their tender ages, they didn't feel badly about doing something a slight bit differently, or looking a slight bit different. I witnessed their maturity growing into something that was beyond their physical age. This process - learning to tell stories with dance movements and facial expressions - had instilled a confidence in them that wouldn't have happened without a combination of their cultural upbringing at home and school, coupled with their story-telling instruction and discipline given them by their guru.

The following images show the students preparing their costumes, dealing with make-up, performing at the Bedford River Festival, and having their formal images captured. See if you can tell the difference in the confidence each of the students shows in these images, from those you've seen in the first part of this book.

Growing Up and Thriving in Two Very Different Cultures

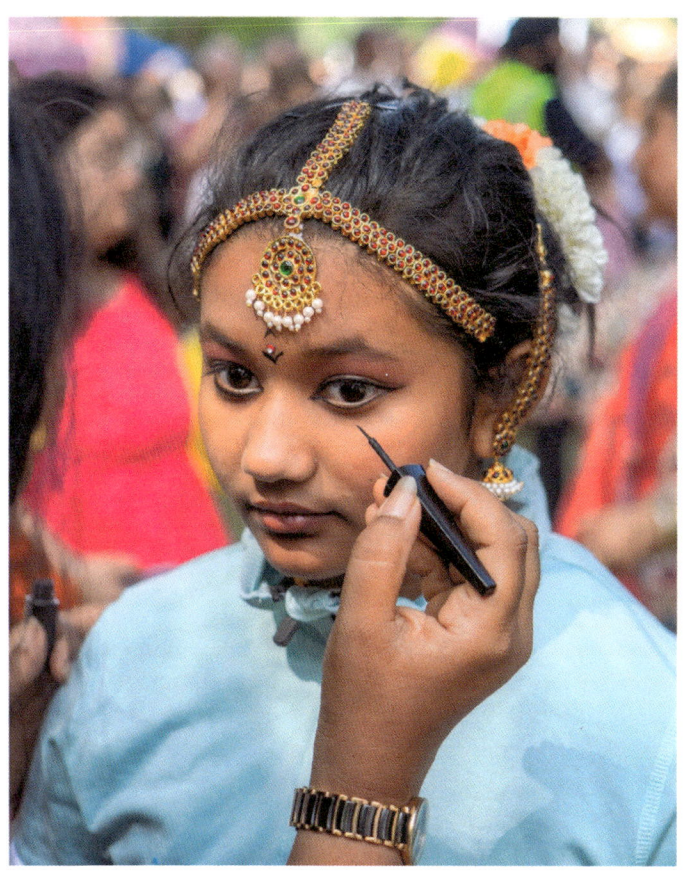

Growing Up and Thriving in Two Very Different Cultures

Growing Up and Thriving in Two Very Different Cultures

Apprehension, concentration and exhilaration were the key words on the day!

Growing Up and Thriving in Two Very Different Cultures

Growing Up and Thriving in Two Very Different Cultures

Growing Up and Thriving in Two Very Different Cultures

Proud and confident students and the guru who made all this happen.

Growing Up and Thriving in Two Very Different Cultures

Growing Up and Thriving in Two Very Different Cultures

Growing Up and Thriving in Two Very Different Cultures

Chaos and noise all around, everyone moving quickly to and fro, but intense concentration reigns supreme with this student.

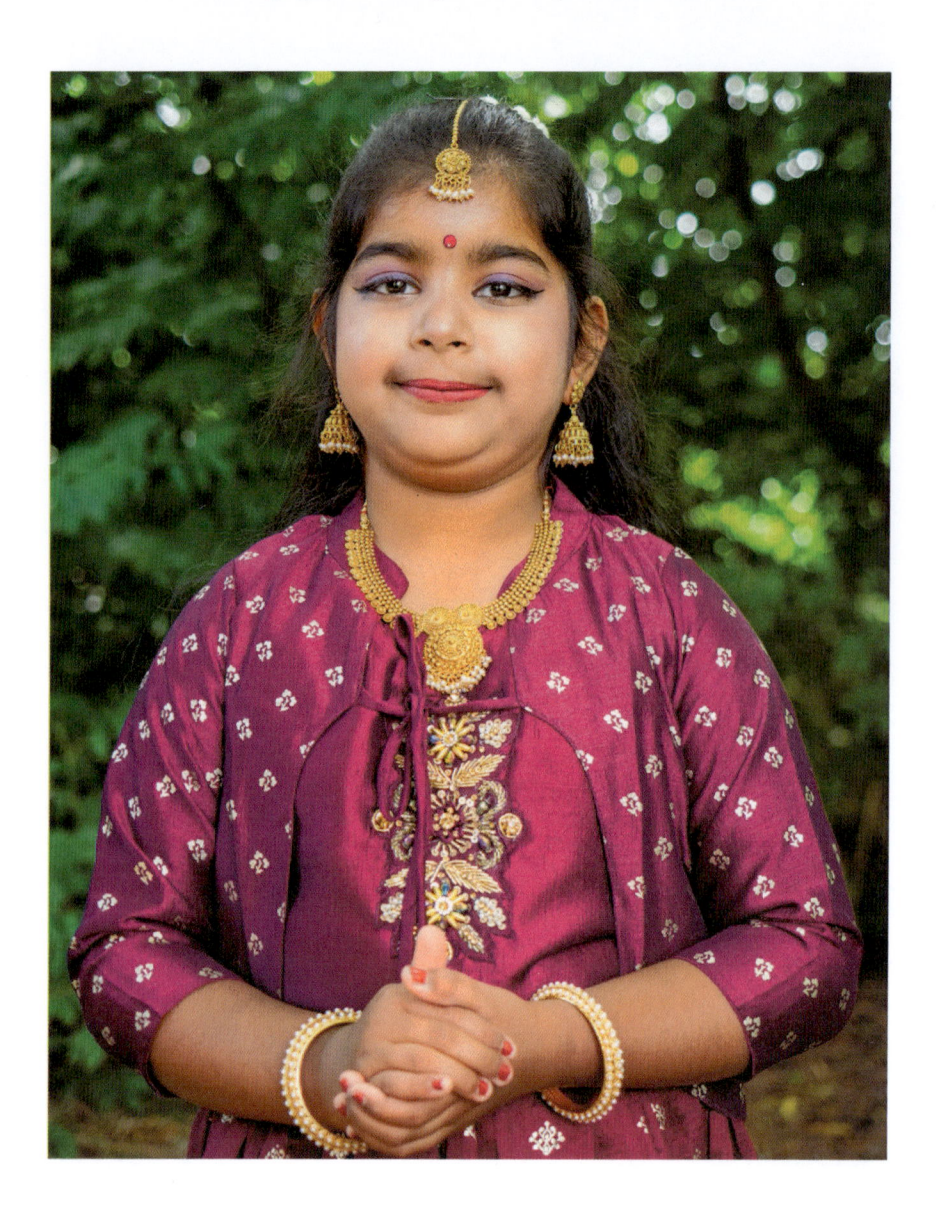

Growing Up and Thriving in Two Very Different Cultures

Growing Up and Thriving in Two Very Different Cultures

Growing Up and Thriving in Two Very Different Cultures

Growing Up and Thriving in Two Very Different Cultures

Growing Up and Thriving in Two Very Different Cultures

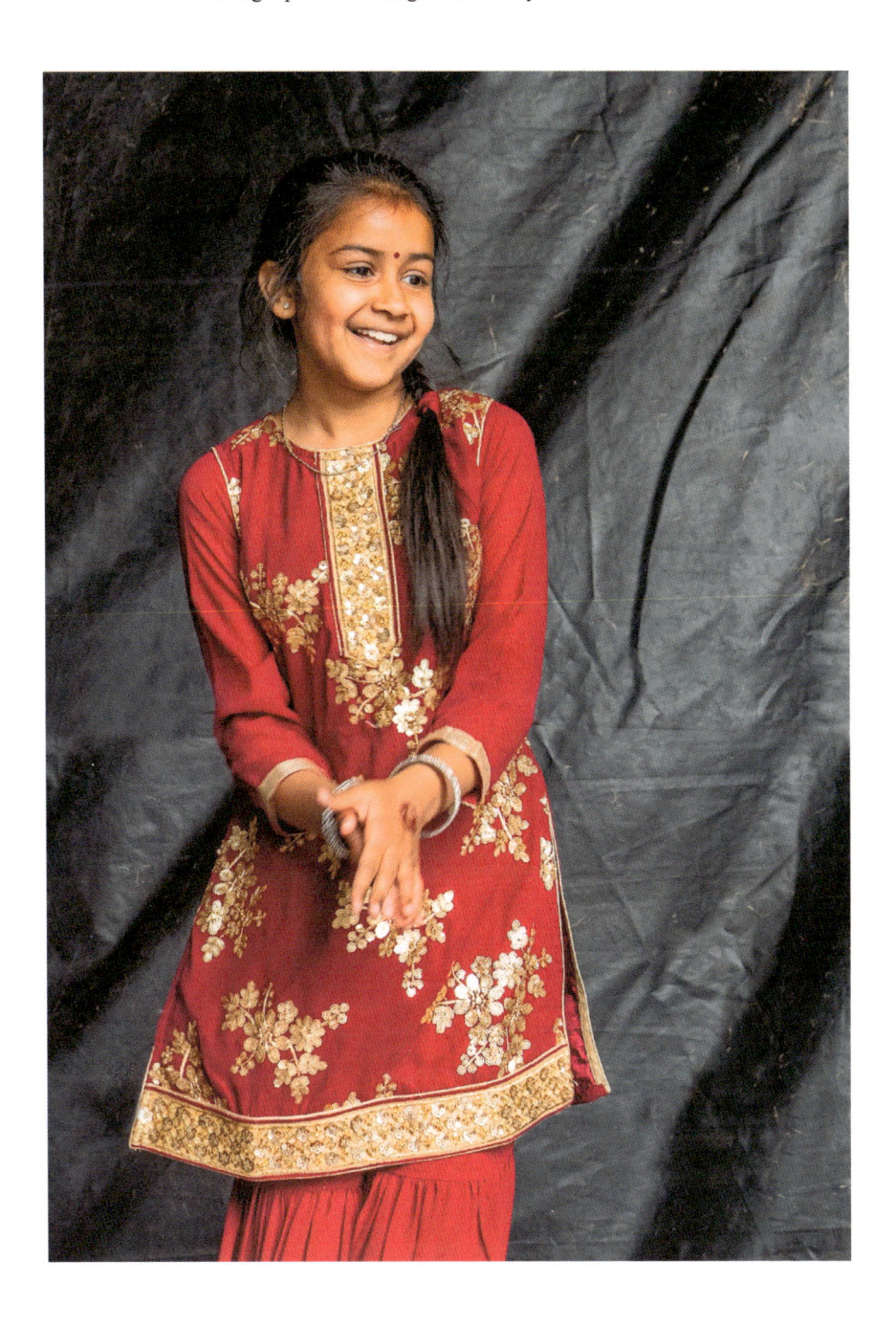

Growing Up and Thriving in Two Very Different Cultures

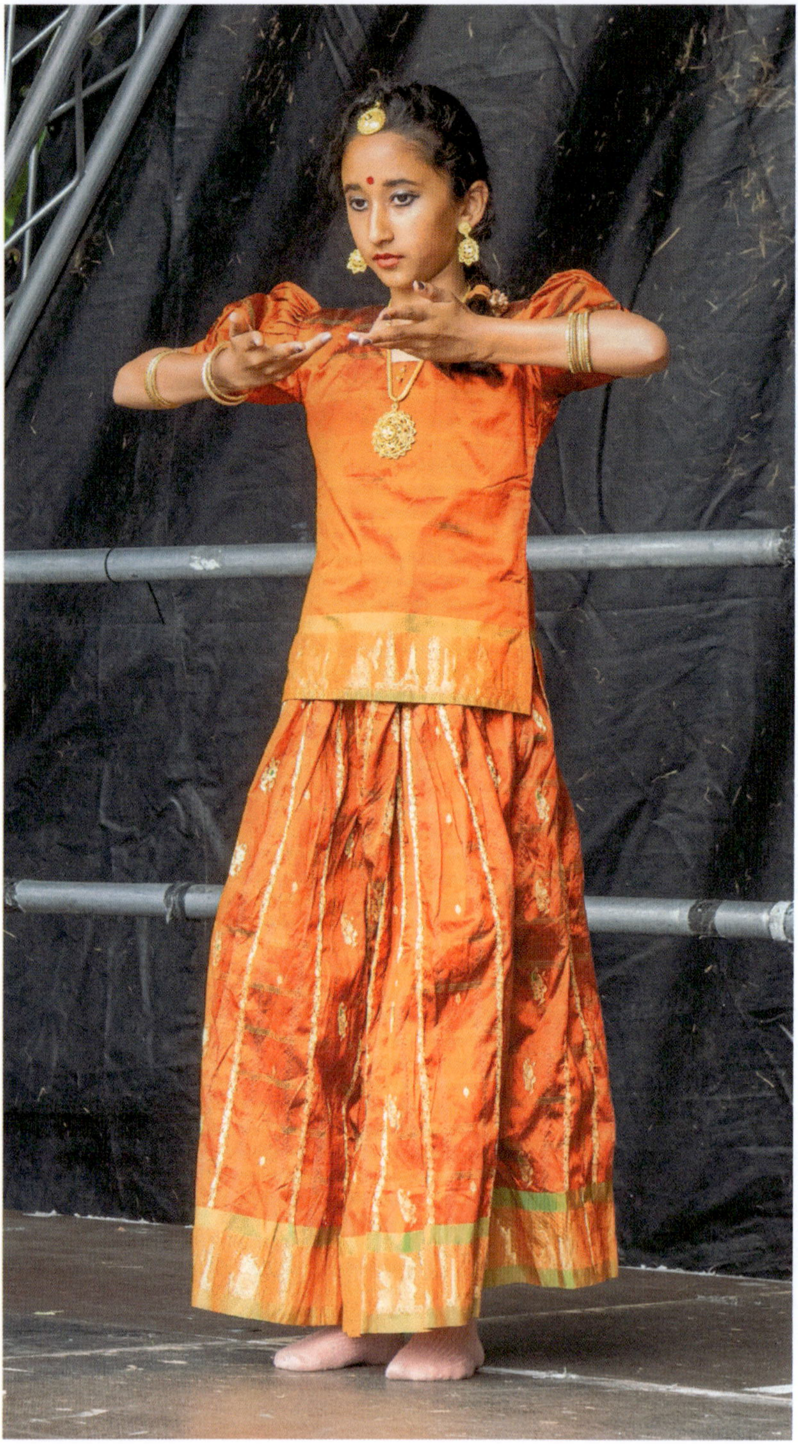

Growing Up and Thriving in Two Very Different Cultures

Proud mum looking on as her daughter demonstrates some intricate moves and gestures.

Growing Up and Thriving in Two Very Different Cultures

Growing Up and Thriving in Two Very Different Cultures

Growing Up and Thriving in Two Very Different Cultures

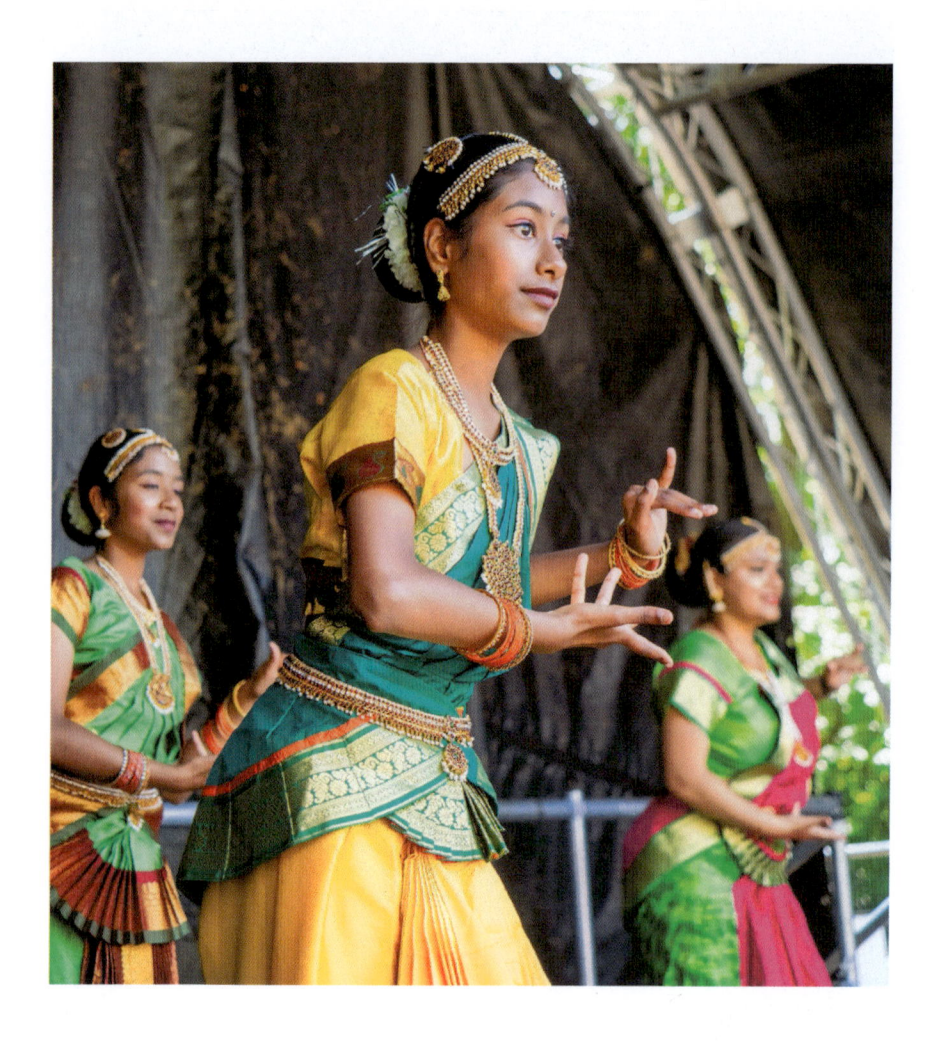

Growing Up and Thriving in Two Very Different Cultures

Growing Up and Thriving in Two Very Different Cultures

Growing Up and Thriving in Two Very Different Cultures

Growing Up and Thriving in Two Very Different Cultures

Growing Up and Thriving in Two Very Different Cultures

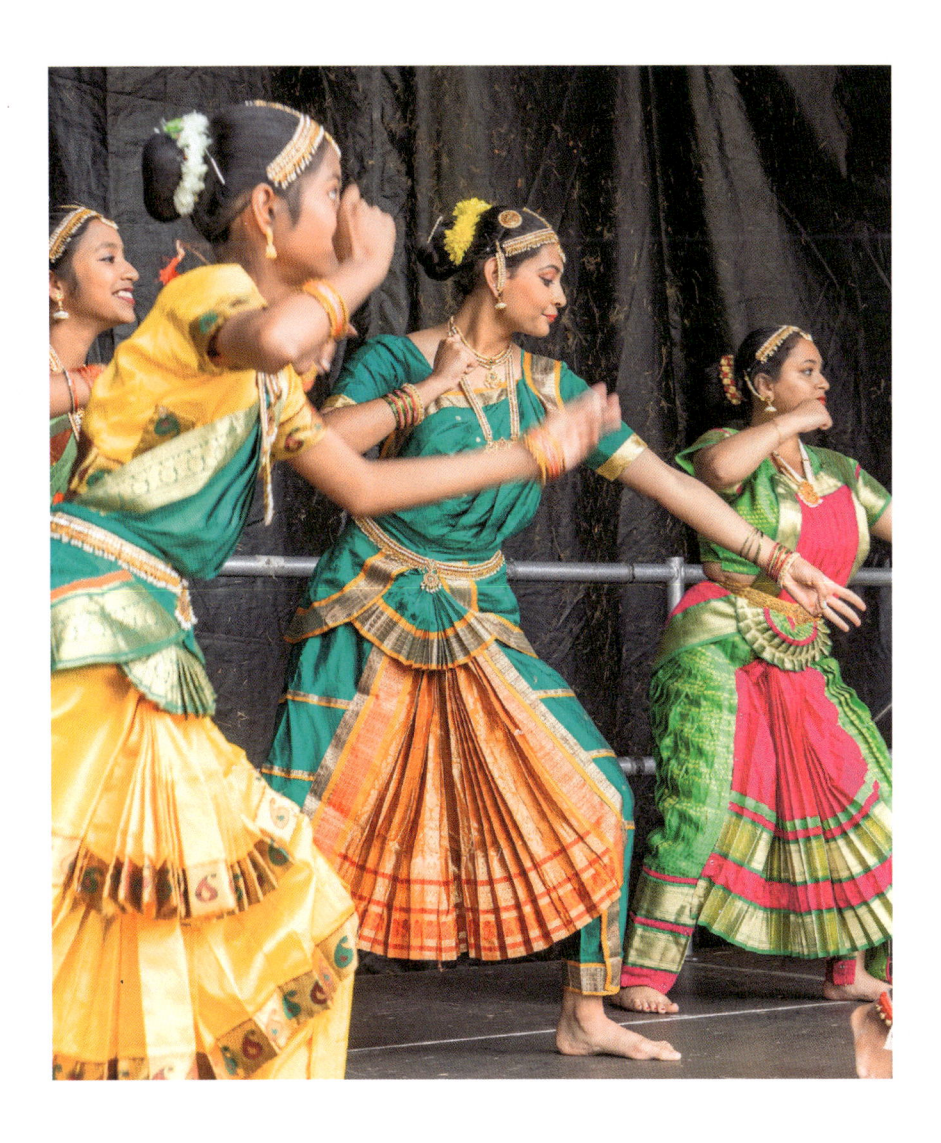

Growing Up and Thriving in Two Very Different Cultures

Growing Up and Thriving in Two Very Different Cultures

Growing Up and Thriving in Two Very Different Cultures

Growing Up and Thriving in Two Very Different Cultures

Watching friends and fellow students perform, from the sidelines.

Growing Up and Thriving in Two Very Different Cultures

Growing Up and Thriving in Two Very Different Cultures

A "decisive nanosecond moment" caught as some of the students transition between their Indian culture and the current British culture!

Growing Up and Thriving in Two Very Different Cultures

This is Saachi, one of the students. She was performing a solo dance, and was flawless in its execution. After she was finished, she apologized to her guru, Sujatha, for not getting the routine she'd been taught, exactly correct. "I got lost in the dance, and just improvised the ending!" Sujatha said she recognized that, and congratulated her for doing just that.

Growing Up and Thriving in Two Very Different Cultures

Backstage she was talking with another student about her routine, and watching from the sidelines was a younger student who idolized these two. They noticed, and what followed was truly special, and indicative of what their culture teaches them.

The two dancers approached the young student, talking softly to her, telling her what a wonderful routine she had just performed, and that she would be a star someday. Notice the one student actually leaning down to talk *to* the younger one, not *at* her? And the expression on her face was beyond priceless; I was lucky to capture a truly decisive moment in that youngster's life…

Preparing for their graduation ceremonies, some final touch-up of make-up, dress positioning, correct poses and the like. This was a time when more formal photos of the graduating students were taken, and what the viewer doesn't see in these is all the people who were there to make their day a very special one!

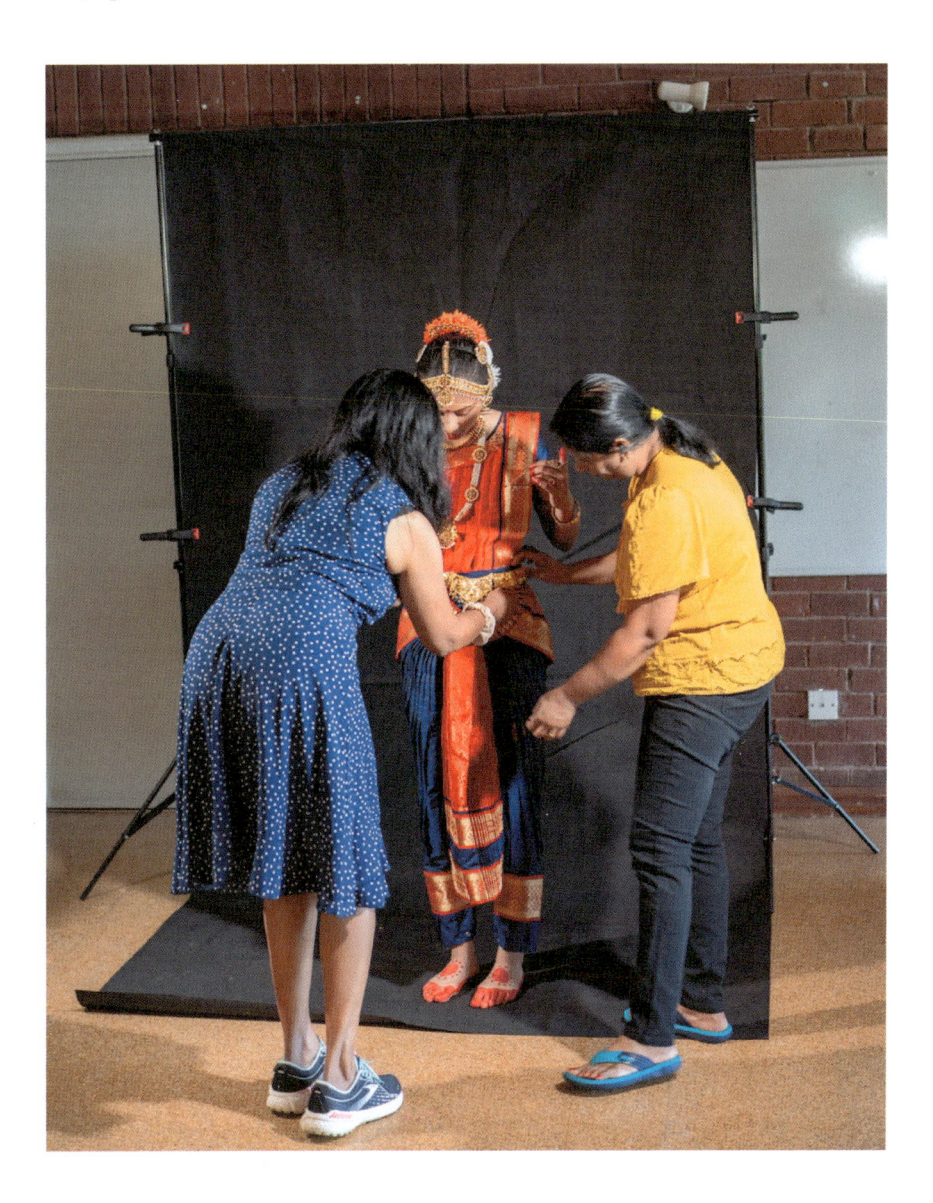

Growing Up and Thriving in Two Very Different Cultures

Growing Up and Thriving in Two Very Different Cultures

Growing Up and Thriving in Two Very Different Cultures

Growing Up and Thriving in Two Very Different Cultures

Growing Up and Thriving in Two Very Different Cultures

Growing Up and Thriving in Two Very Different Cultures

Growing Up and Thriving in Two Very Different Cultures

Growing Up and Thriving in Two Very Different Cultures

Growing Up and Thriving in Two Very Different Cultures

Growing Up and Thriving in Two Very Different Cultures

Growing Up and Thriving in Two Very Different Cultures

Growing Up and Thriving in Two Very Different Cultures

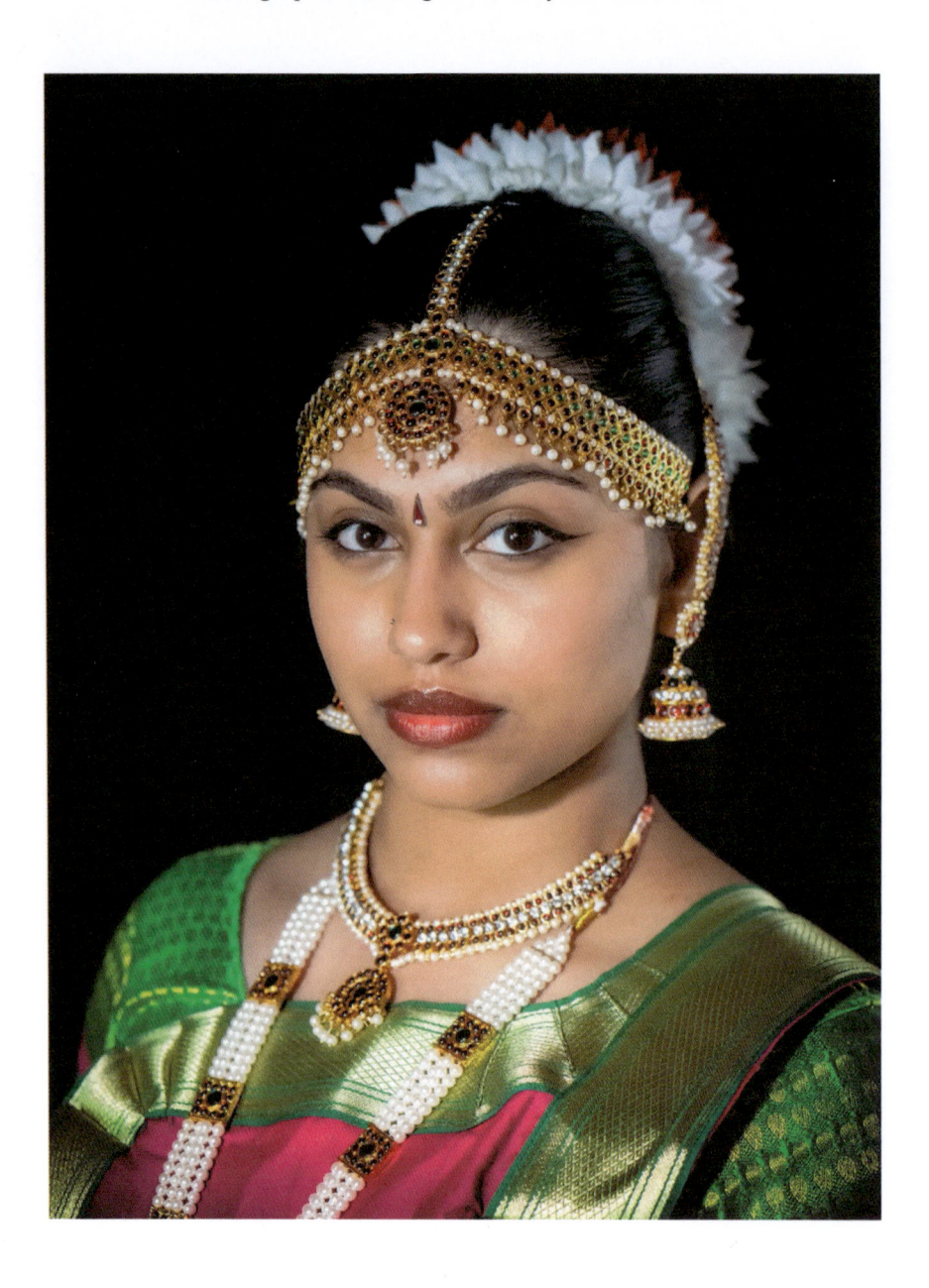

Growing Up and Thriving in Two Very Different Cultures

Growing Up and Thriving in Two Very Different Cultures

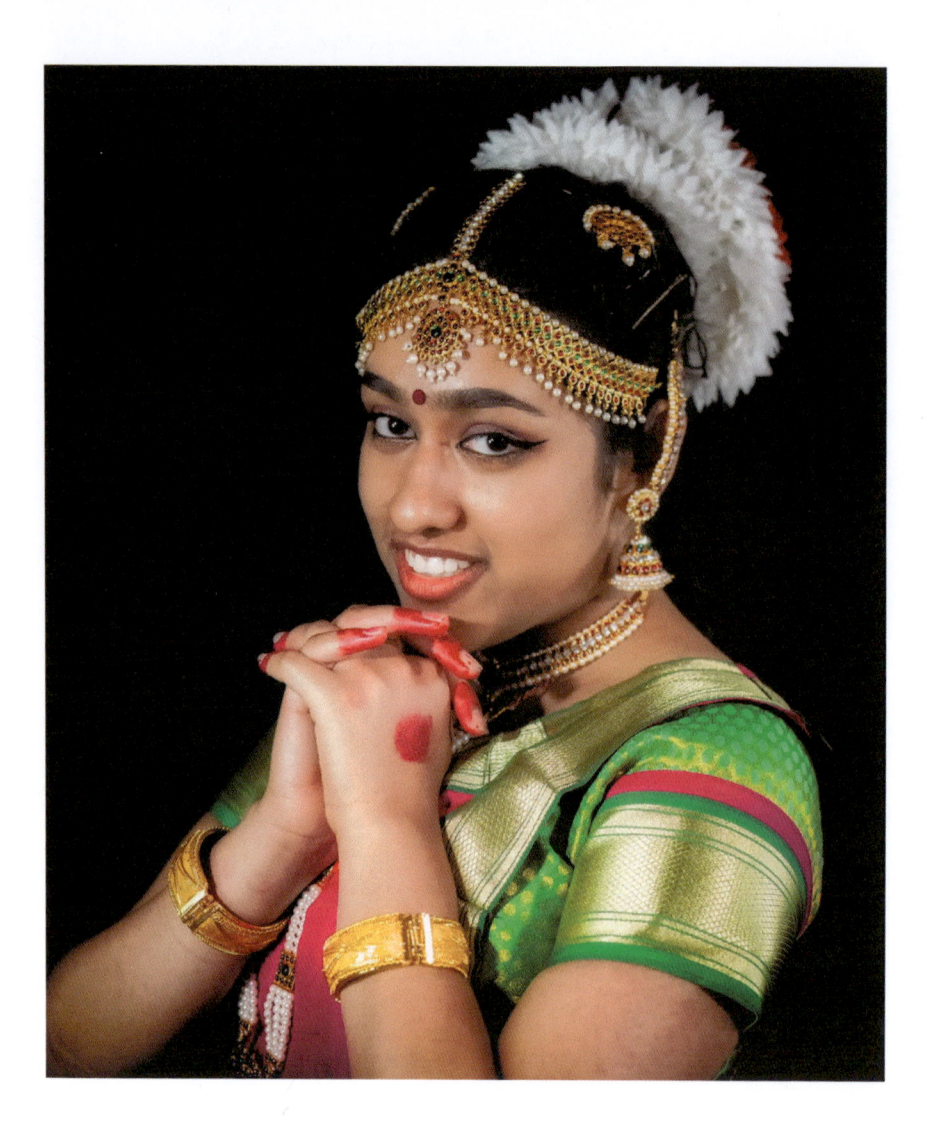

Growing Up and Thriving in Two Very Different Cultures

Growing Up and Thriving in Two Very Different Cultures

Guru Sujatha Chenilath

6 GRADUATION DAYS

After some students have been studying and practicing the art of Classical Indian Dancing for ten years or even longer, they are ready to graduate from the courses and demonstrate to the world how well they've done in those studies.

The following images were captured at three graduation ceremonies over a period of one year. I witnessed ceremonies that had audiences of nearly 500 family members, friends and interested members of the public at large, while others were more intimate affairs with only 150 or so.

These students were immensely proud of their accomplishments, and of course their family and friends were delighted with the results. The images show that dedication, accomplishment and pride.

Please enjoy the chaos, turmoil and joy of graduation day!

Growing Up and Thriving in Two Very Different Cultures

Growing Up and Thriving in Two Very Different Cultures

Growing Up and Thriving in Two Very Different Cultures

Growing Up and Thriving in Two Very Different Cultures

Growing Up and Thriving in Two Very Different Cultures

Guru Sujatha Chenilath speaking to an overflow crowd at the first graduation I witnessed.

Proud graduating class! Swelling with pride!

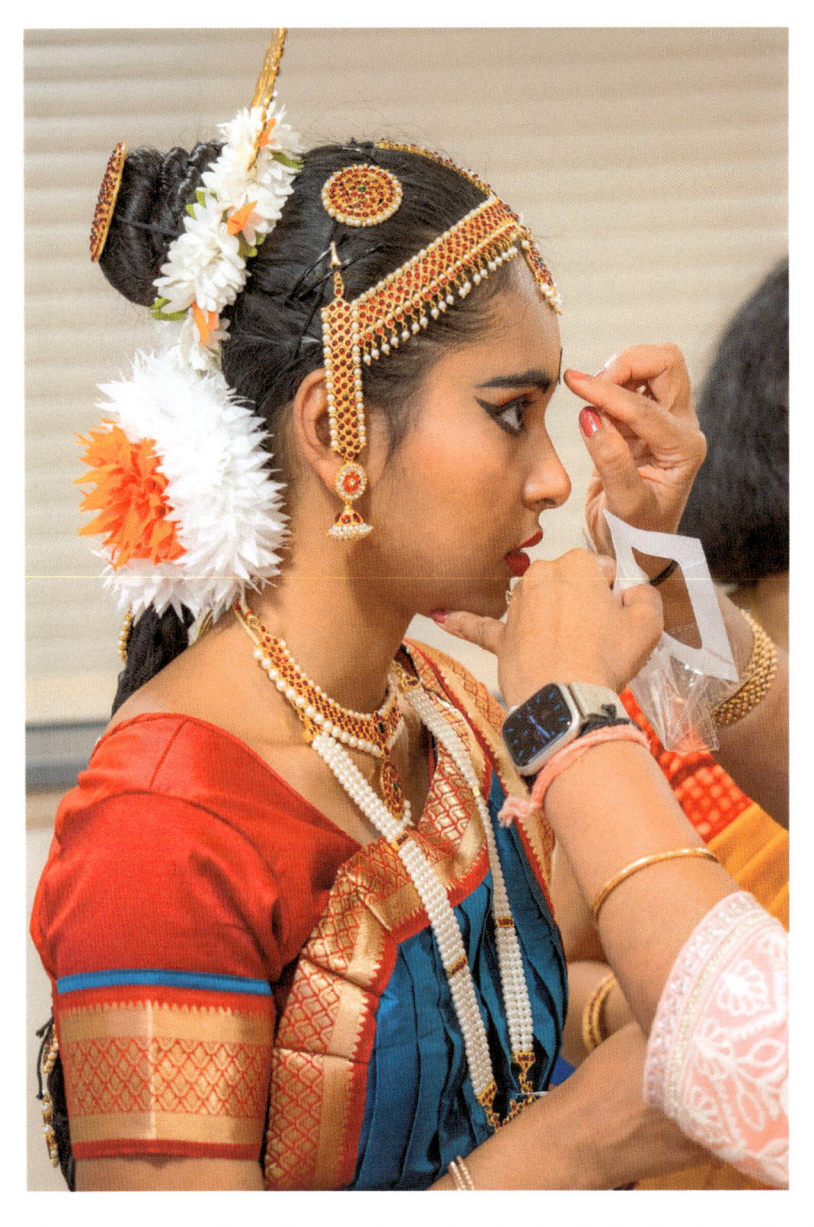

Growing Up and Thriving in Two Very Different Cultures

Final preparations take as long as they take! Getting it absolutely perfect is what's happening in the next several pages.

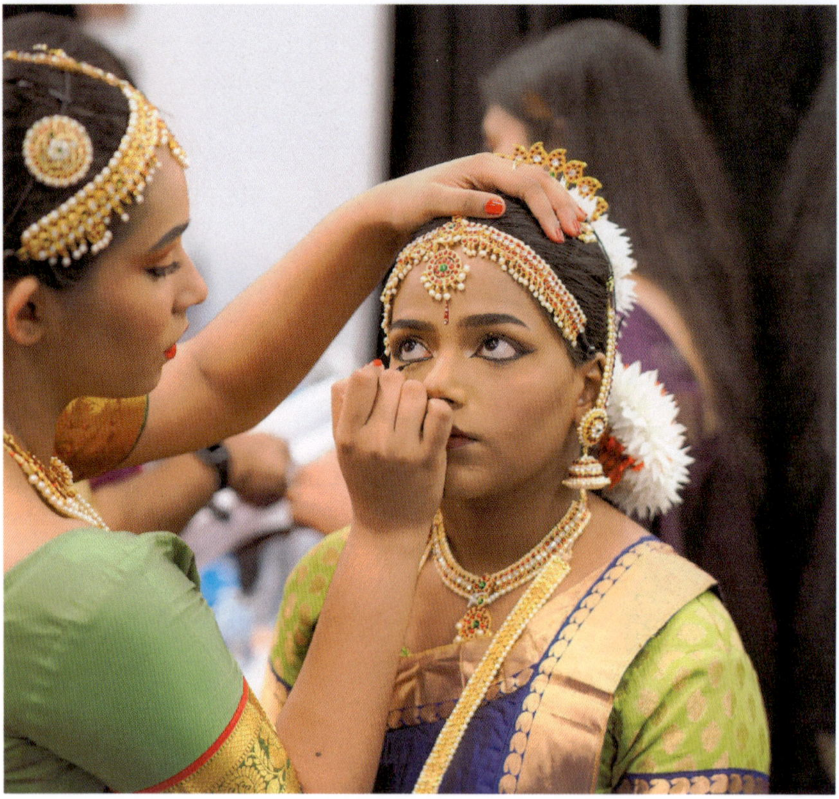

Growing Up and Thriving in Two Very Different Cultures

Growing Up and Thriving in Two Very Different Cultures

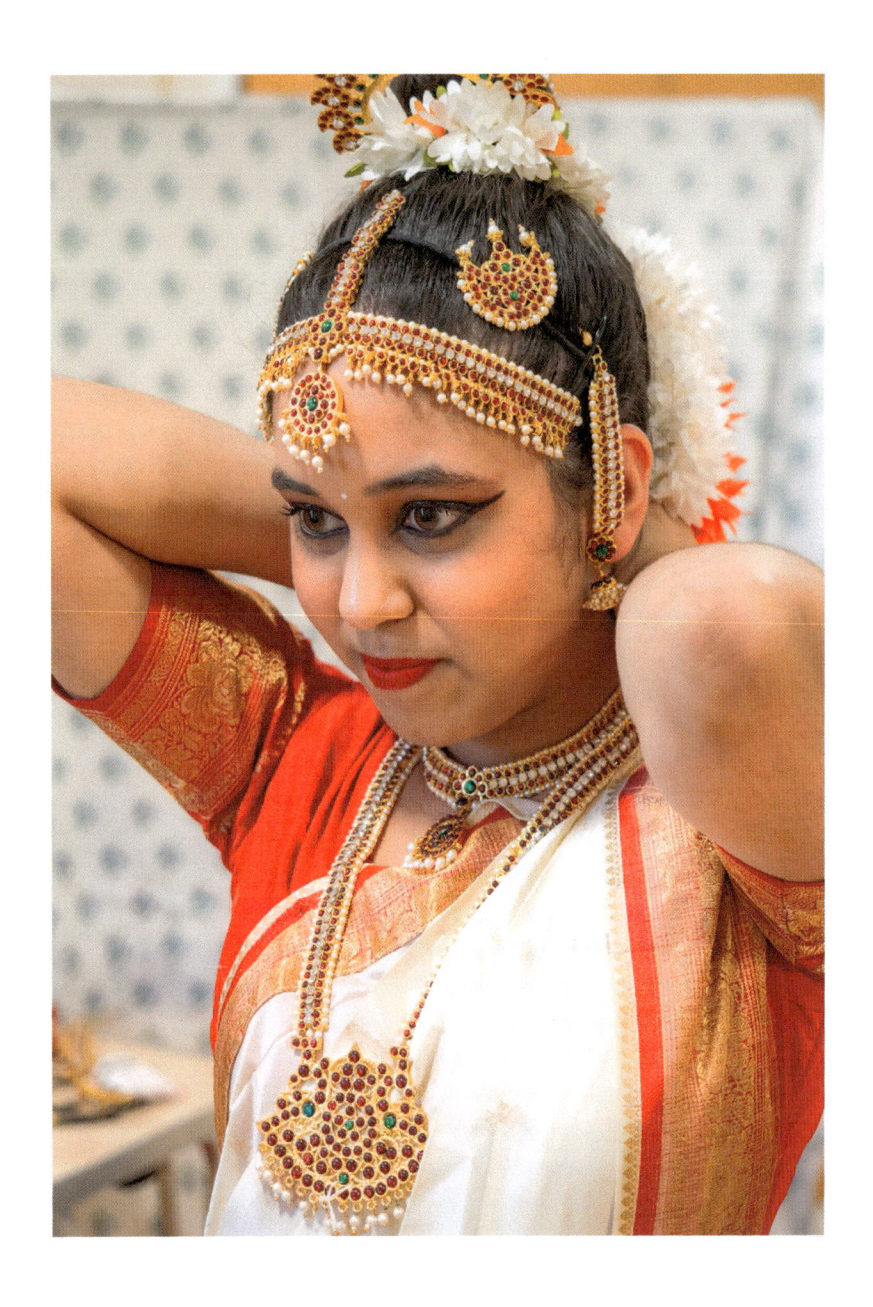

Growing Up and Thriving in Two Very Different Cultures

Growing Up and Thriving in Two Very Different Cultures

Growing Up and Thriving in Two Very Different Cultures

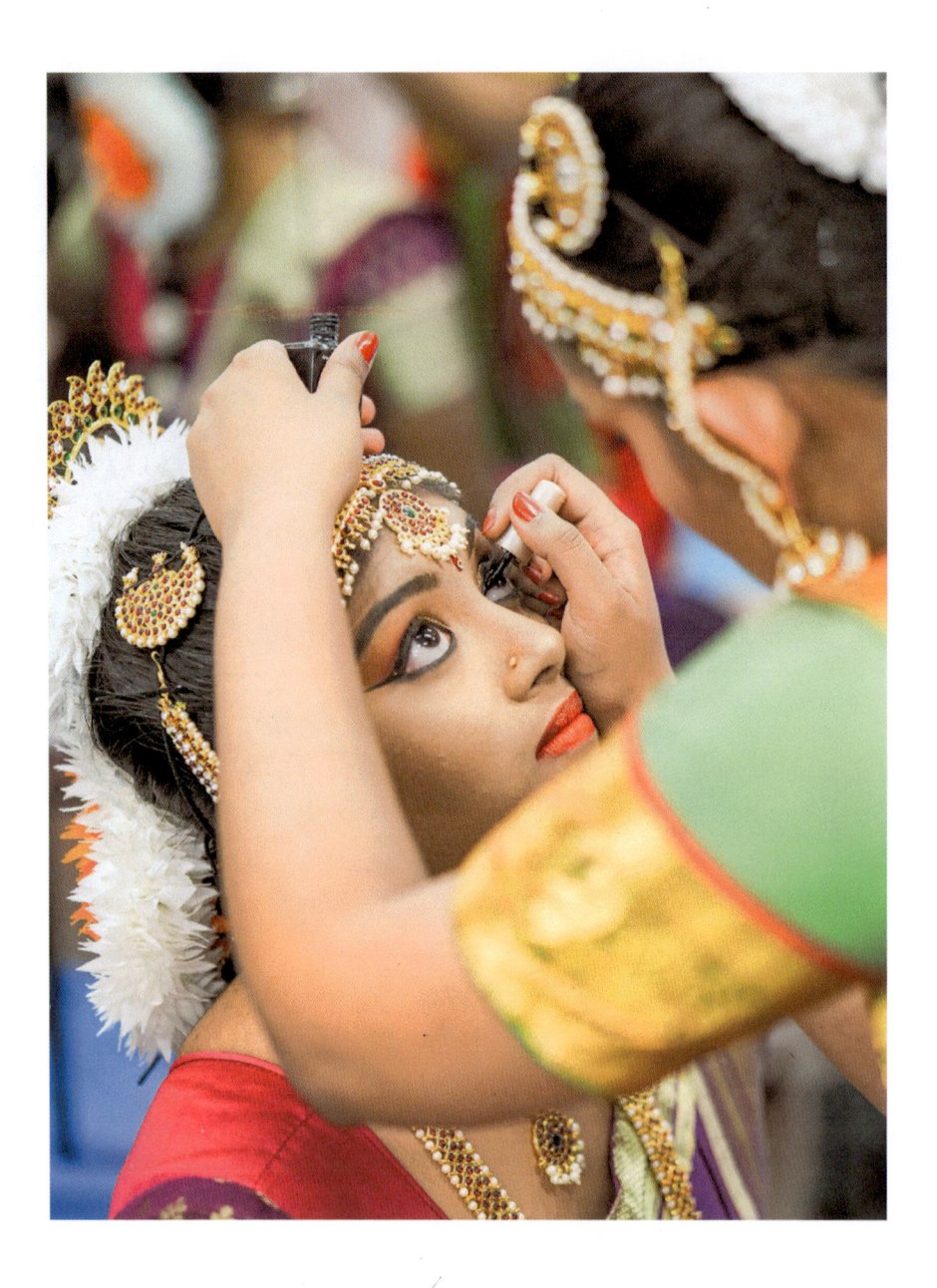

Growing Up and Thriving in Two Very Different Cultures

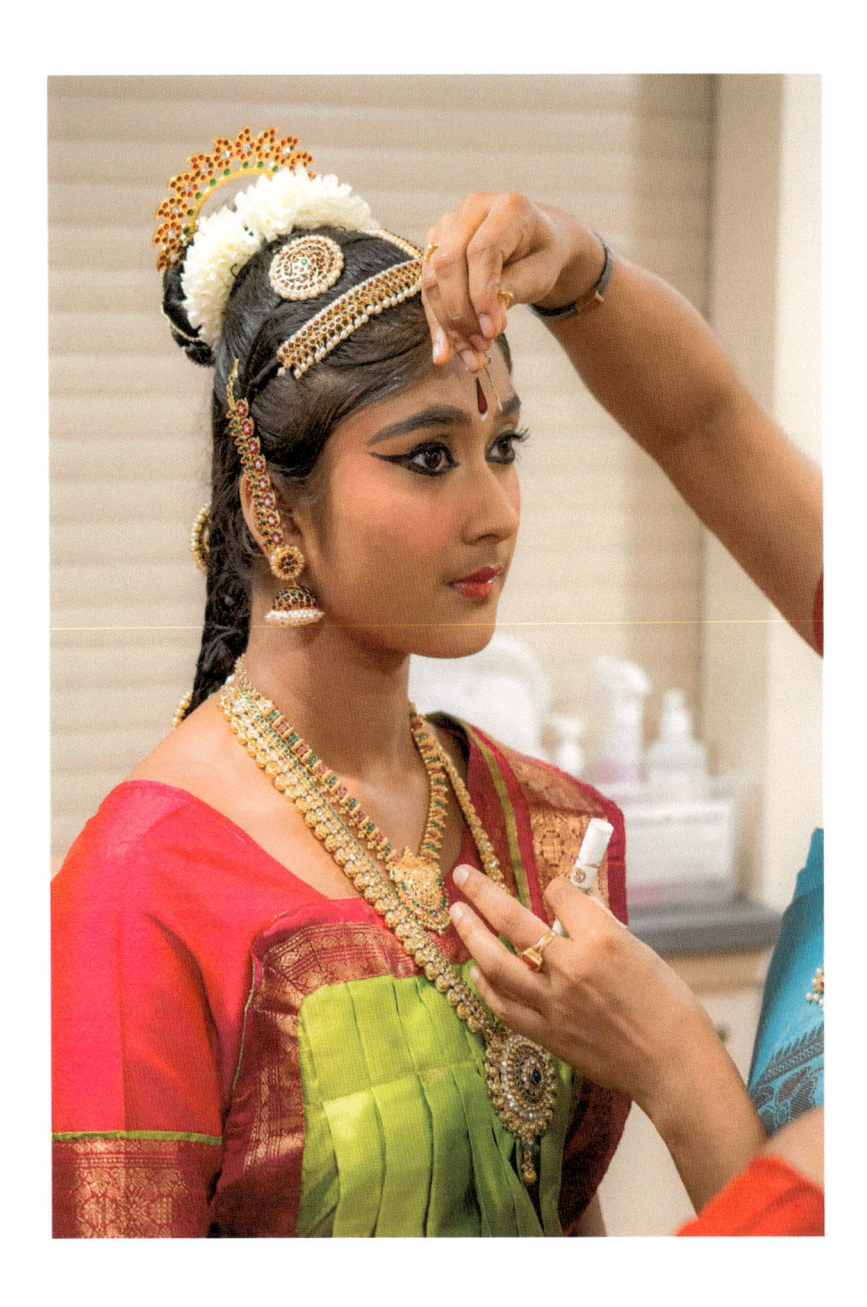

Growing Up and Thriving in Two Very Different Cultures

Growing Up and Thriving in Two Very Different Cultures

Growing Up and Thriving in Two Very Different Cultures

Growing Up and Thriving in Two Very Different Cultures

More glowing graduates!

Growing Up and Thriving in Two Very Different Cultures

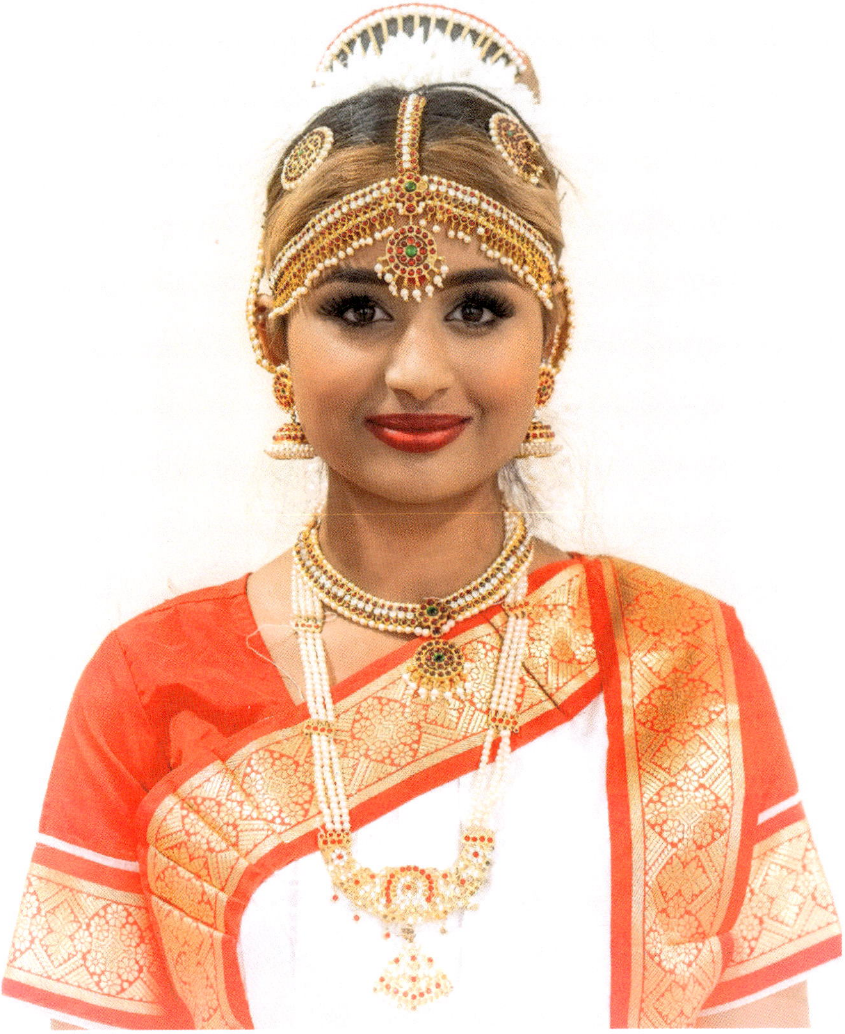

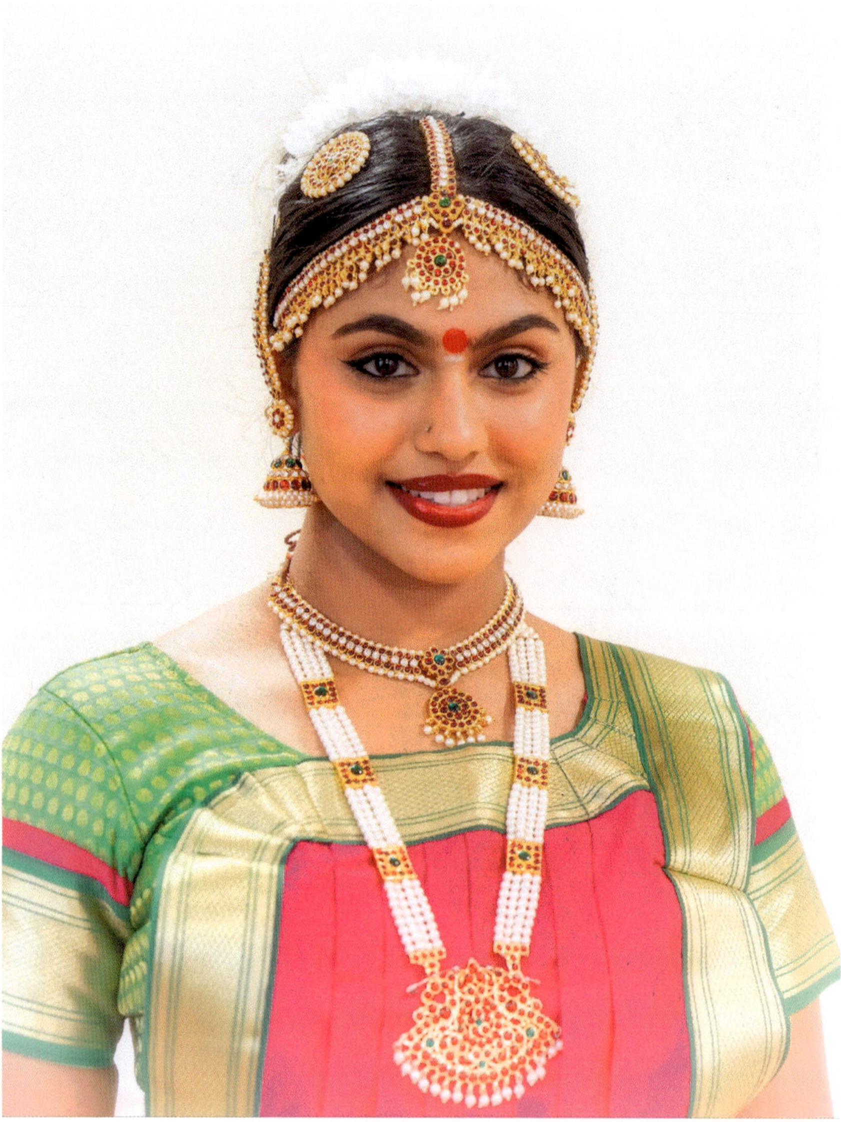

Growing Up and Thriving in Two Very Different Cultures

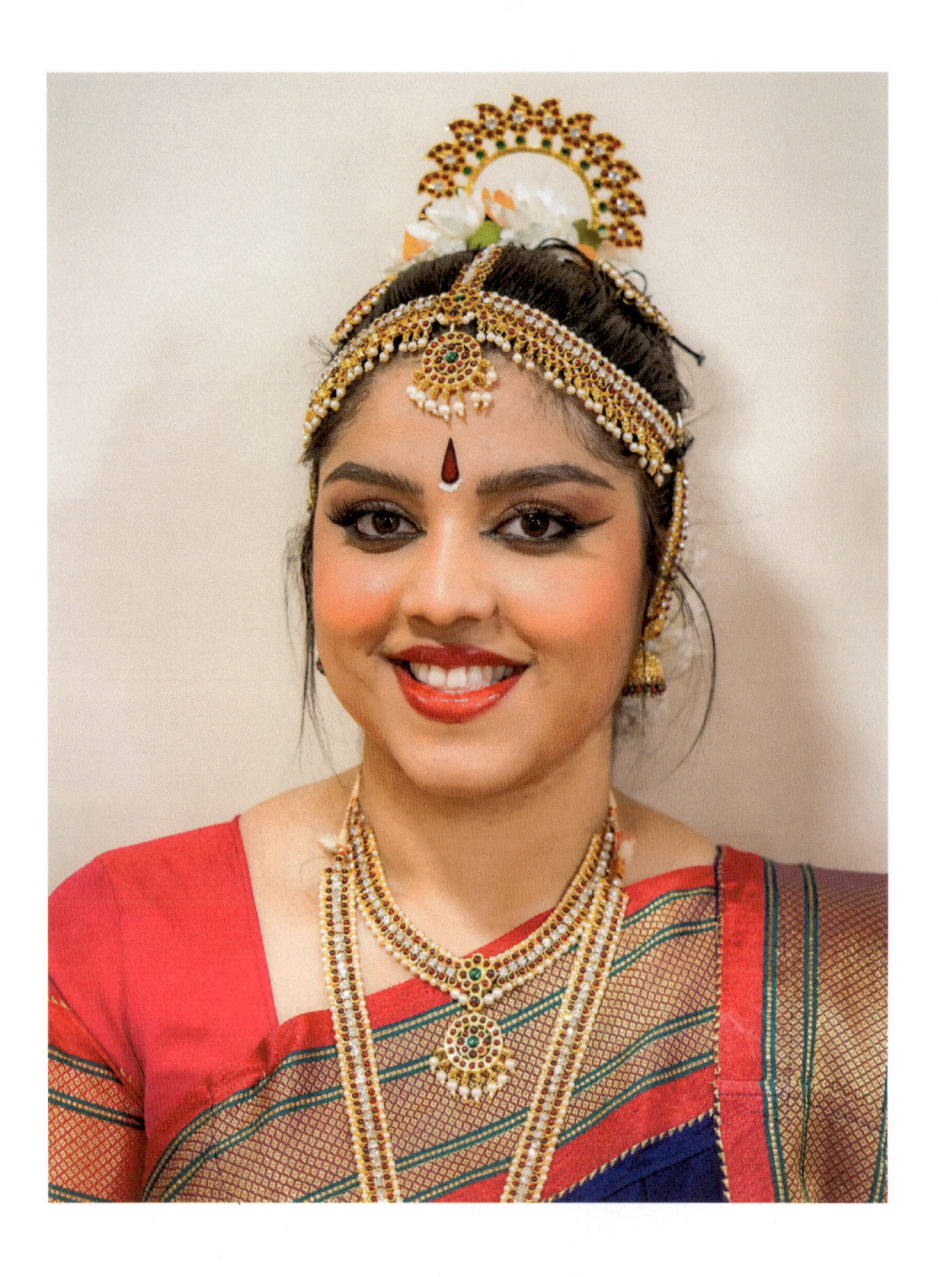

Growing Up and Thriving in Two Very Different Cultures

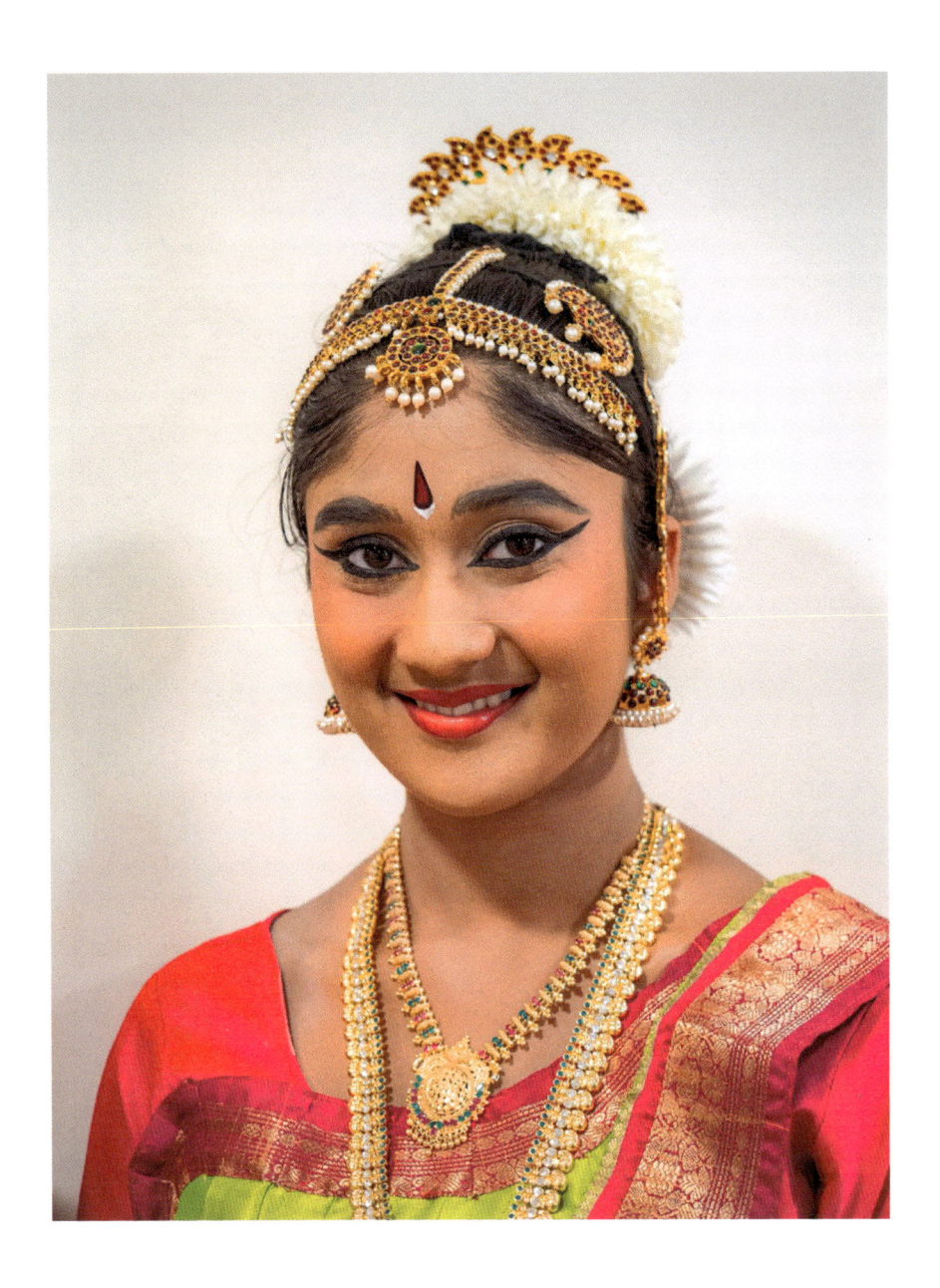

Growing Up and Thriving in Two Very Different Cultures

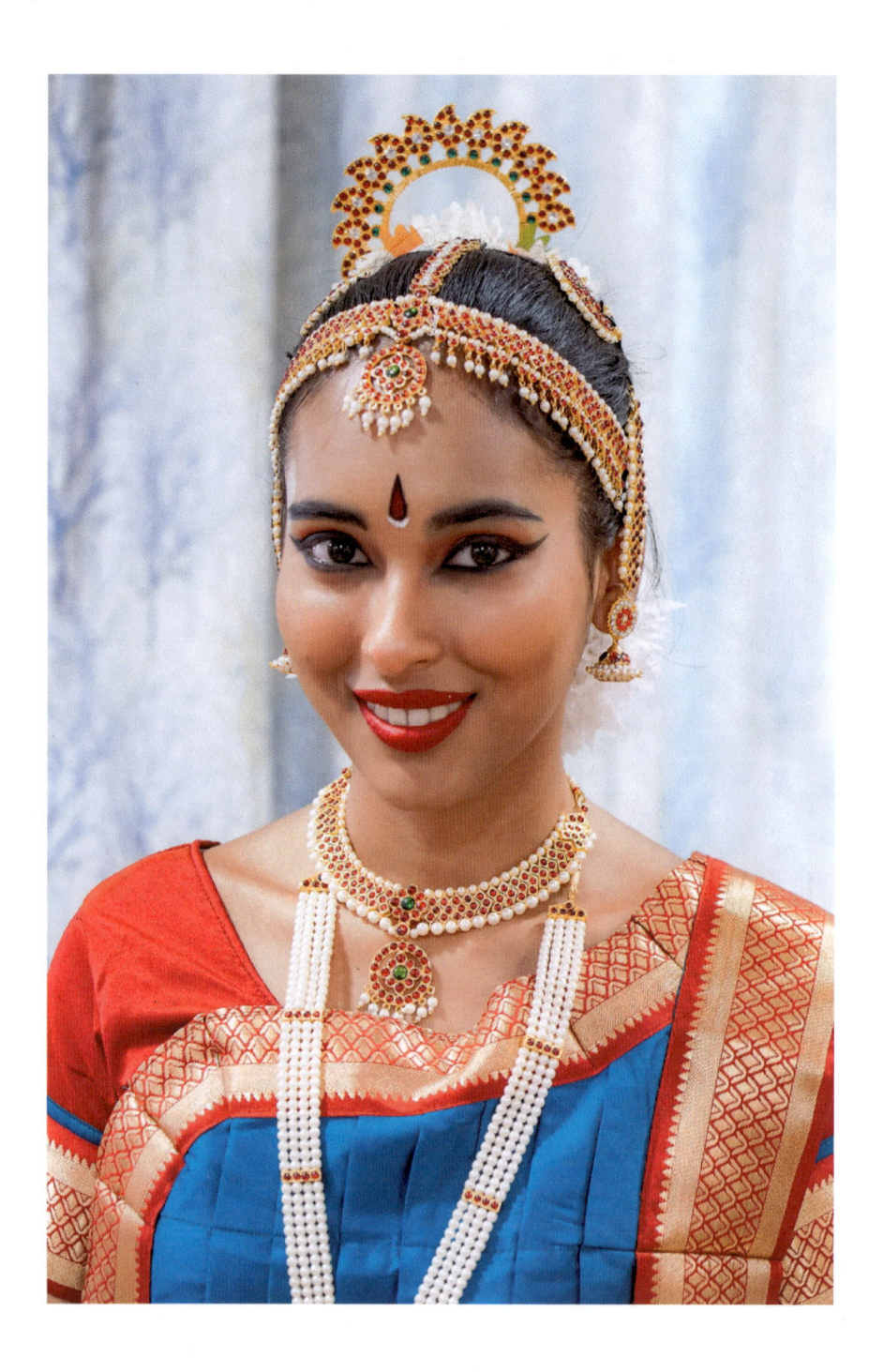

Growing Up and Thriving in Two Very Different Cultures

Growing Up and Thriving in Two Very Different Cultures

Graduating Class Photograph!

Growing Up and Thriving in Two Very Different Cultures

Growing Up and Thriving in Two Very Different Cultures

Growing Up and Thriving in Two Very Different Cultures

Growing Up and Thriving in Two Very Different Cultures

Growing Up and Thriving in Two Very Different Cultures

Growing Up and Thriving in Two Very Different Cultures

Growing Up and Thriving in Two Very Different Cultures

Growing Up and Thriving in Two Very Different Cultures

Growing Up and Thriving in Two Very Different Cultures

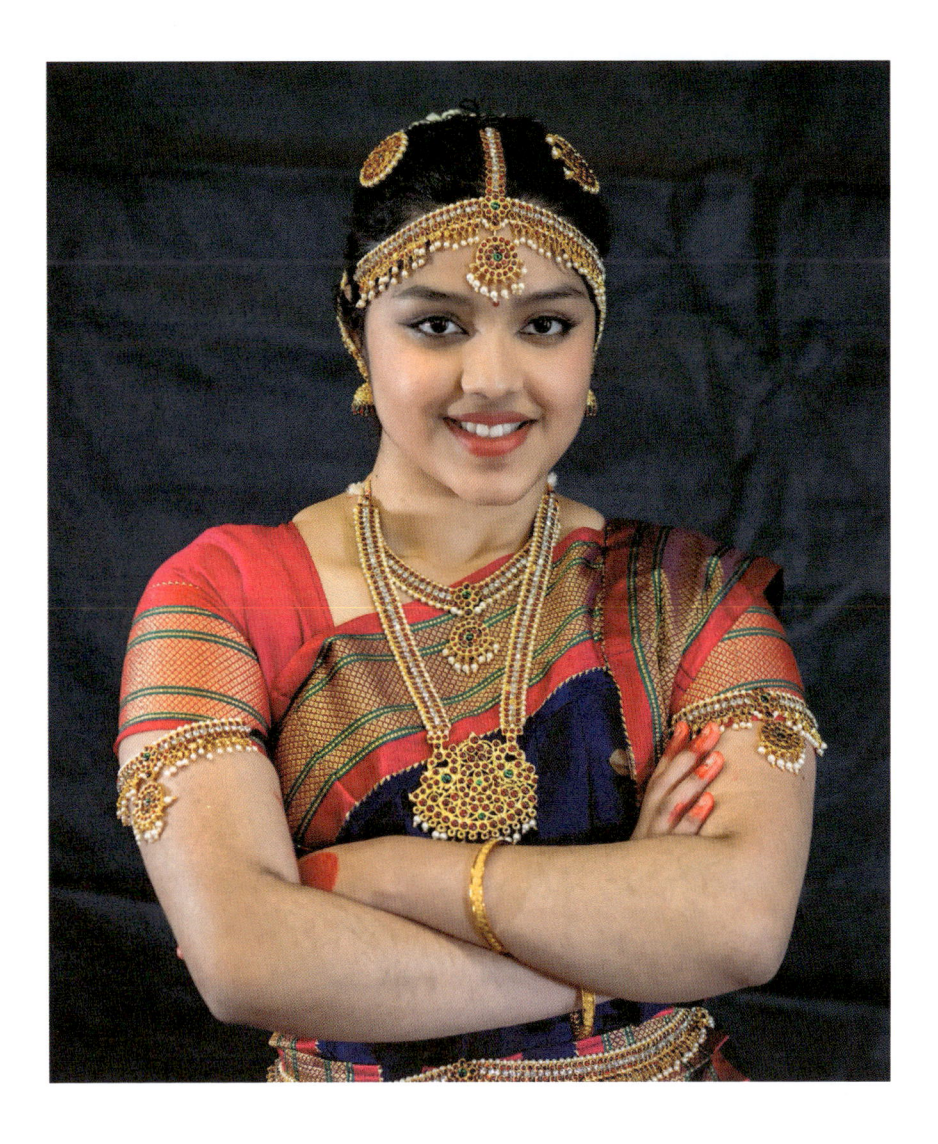

Growing Up and Thriving in Two Very Different Cultures

Growing Up and Thriving in Two Very Different Cultures

Growing Up and Thriving in Two Very Different Cultures

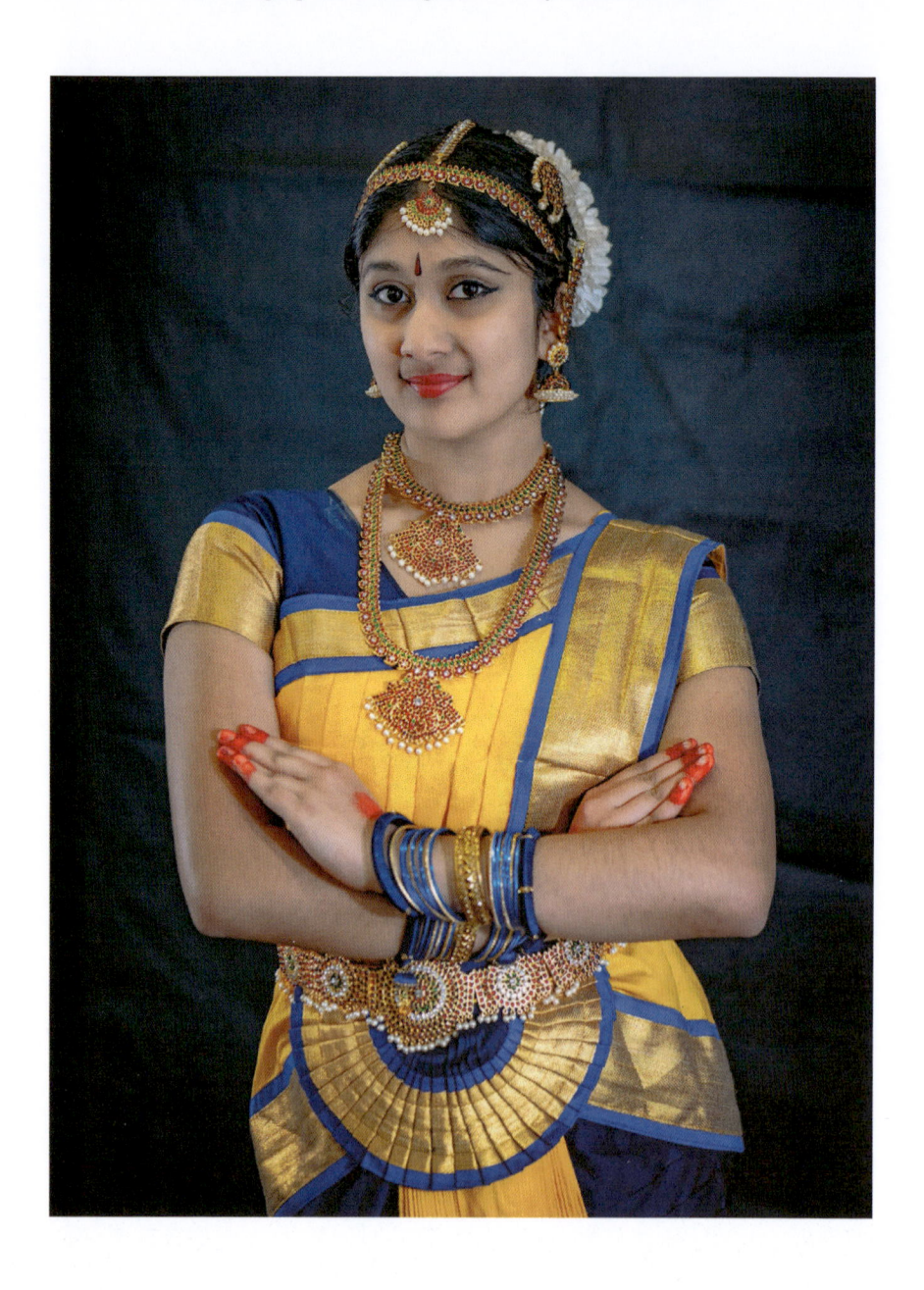

Growing Up and Thriving in Two Very Different Cultures

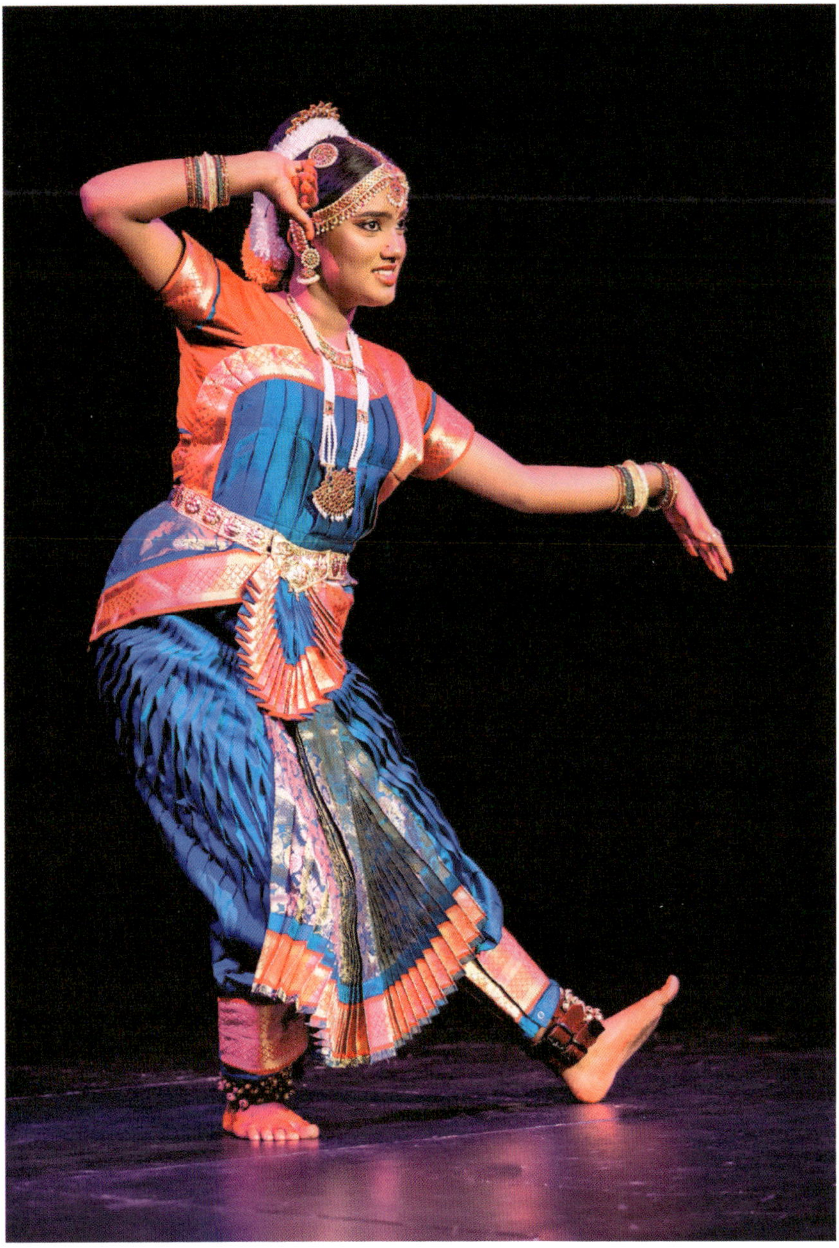

Growing Up and Thriving in Two Very Different Cultures

Growing Up and Thriving in Two Very Different Cultures

Growing Up and Thriving in Two Very Different Cultures

Growing Up and Thriving in Two Very Different Cultures

Growing Up and Thriving in Two Very Different Cultures

Growing Up and Thriving in Two Very Different Cultures

Growing Up and Thriving in Two Very Different Cultures

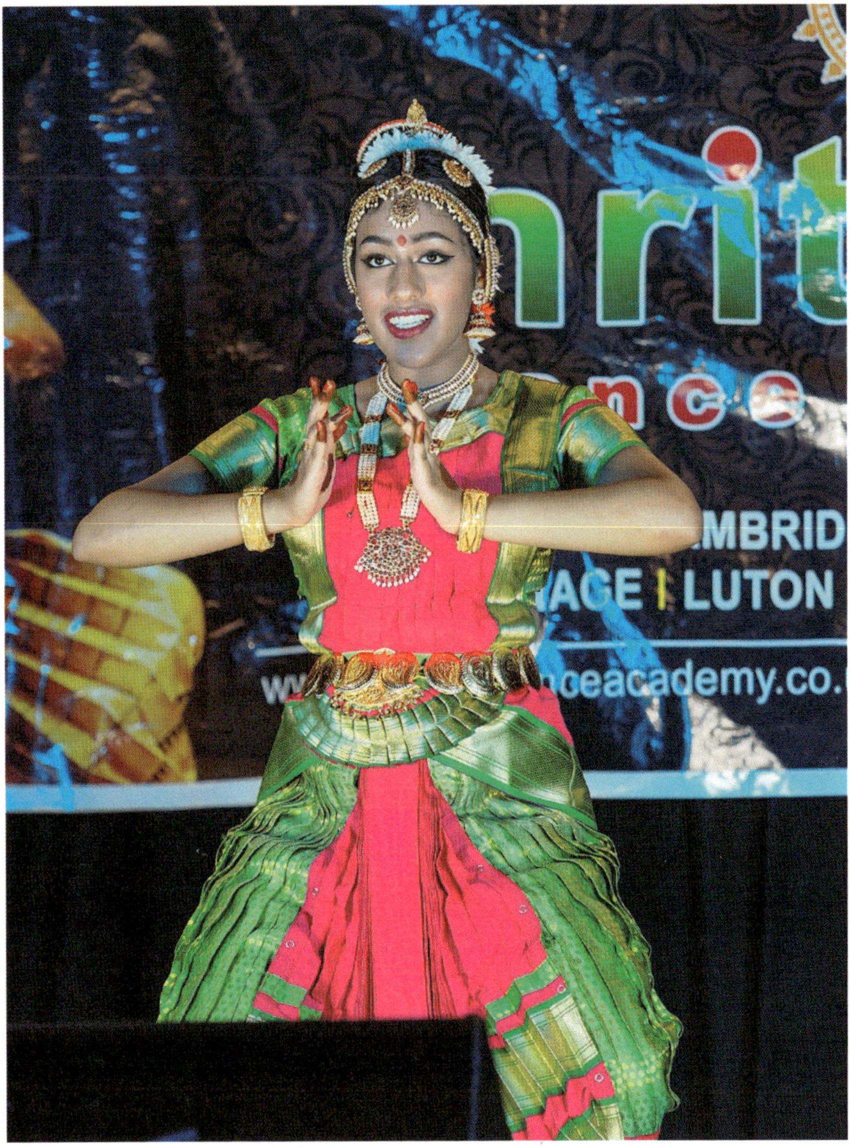
nrit
nce
MBRID
AGE | LUTON
nceacademy.co.

Growing Up and Thriving in Two Very Different Cultures

Growing Up and Thriving in Two Very Different Cultures

Growing Up and Thriving in Two Very Different Cultures

Growing Up and Thriving in Two Very Different Cultures

Above you can see four of the six students who graduated on that day, telling a story of deception, deceit, distress, anger and despair. I was amazed to get any images from this time in the show; I was side stage, the colour of the lighting was all over the place, the movement of the dancers was rapid enough to be a challenge with shutter speed, and of course I had no real idea what the 'story' was about! But in spite of everything I did, this series still turned out just fine!

This is what I consider to be my best image capture of the day. In the story, here was the mother of her son, lying dead at her feet, and she was in total anguish with the circumstances leading up to his death. She was pleading with God to explain it all to her, and to forgive her for forsaking her son. Everything was wrong from a photographic point of view, but I released the shutter at just the right time to capture the emotion, which is always the intent when dealing with storytelling and dance.

Growing Up and Thriving in Two Very Different Cultures

Growing Up and Thriving in Two Very Different Cultures

Growing Up and Thriving in Two Very Different Cultures

Growing Up and Thriving in Two Very Different Cultures

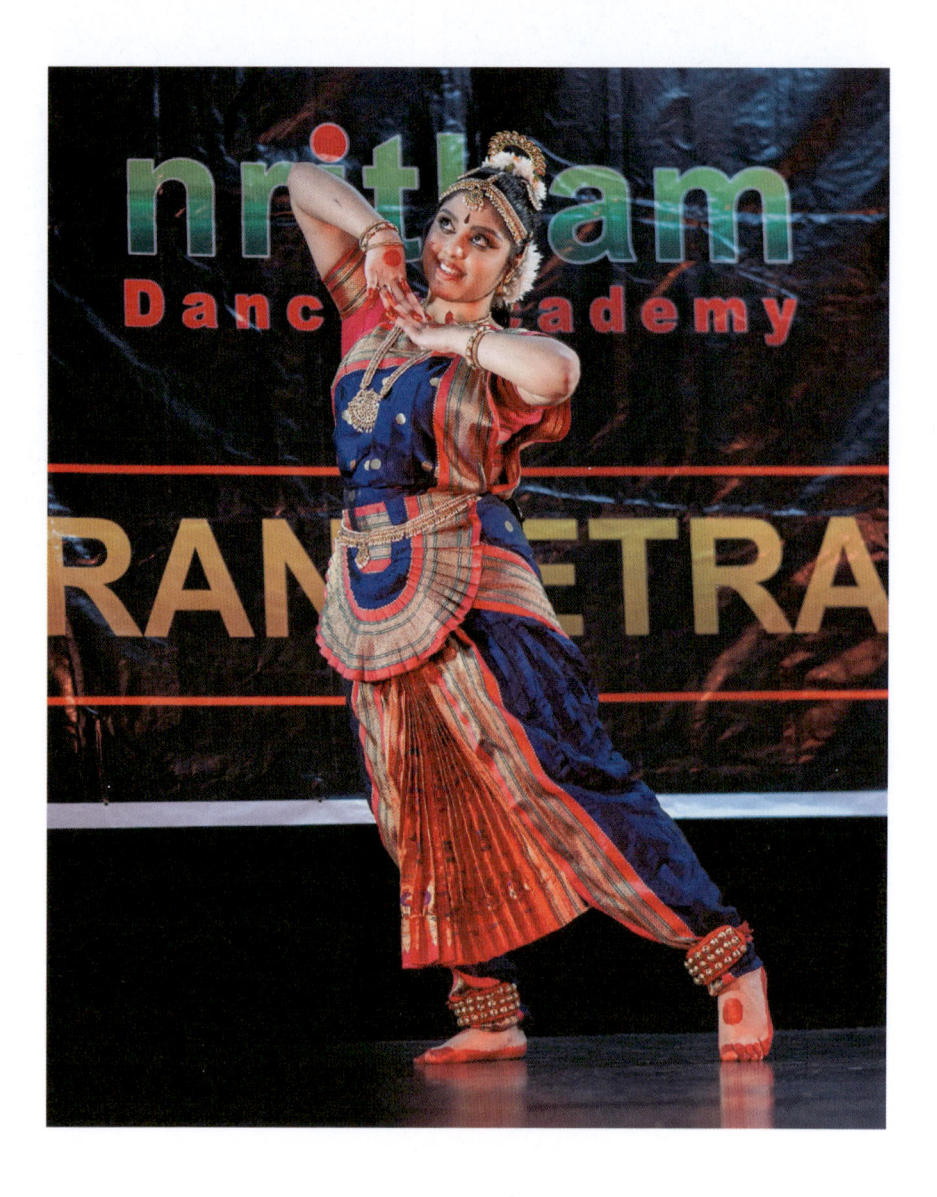

Growing Up and Thriving in Two Very Different Cultures

This is Sreya, the daughter of guru Sujatha, at her graduation. Sreya takes her dancing and storytelling to the limit, such that she apparently forgets there's even a crowd watching her. If you look closely in this image, you can find a tear drop from her left eye, caused as she really got into the story which was, at that point, about loss and anger.

Growing Up and Thriving in Two Very Different Cultures

Growing Up and Thriving in Two Very Different Cultures

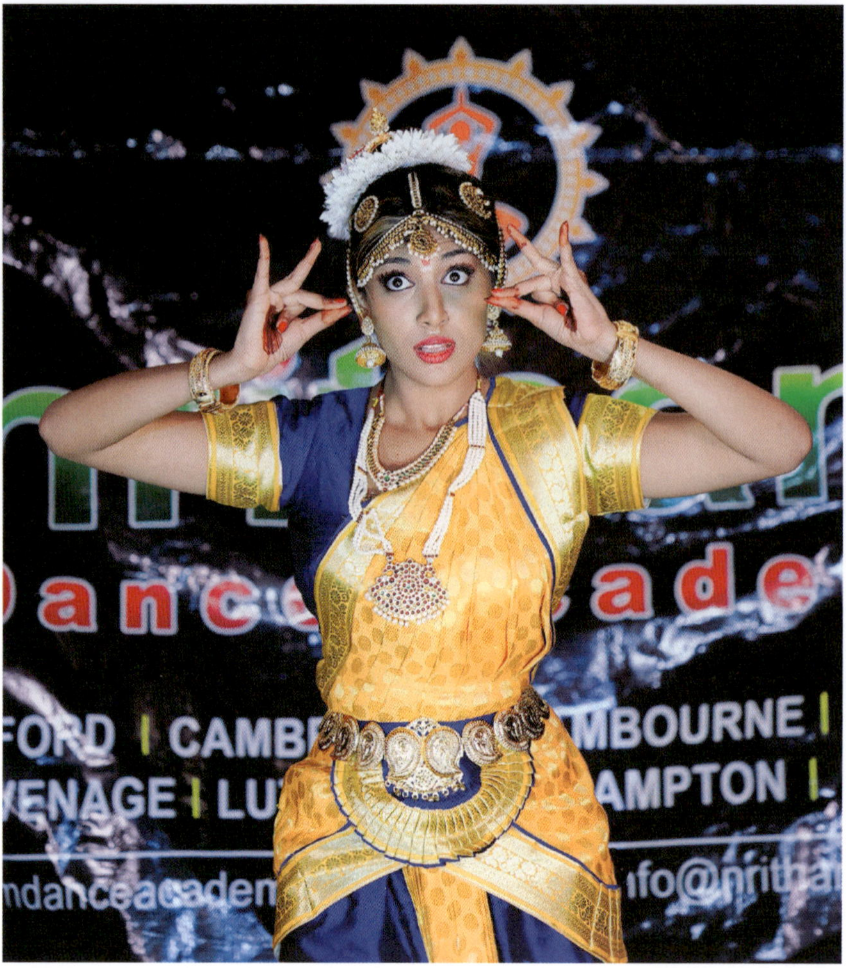

Growing Up and Thriving in Two Very Different Cultures

Growing Up and Thriving in Two Very Different Cultures

Growing Up and Thriving in Two Very Different Cultures

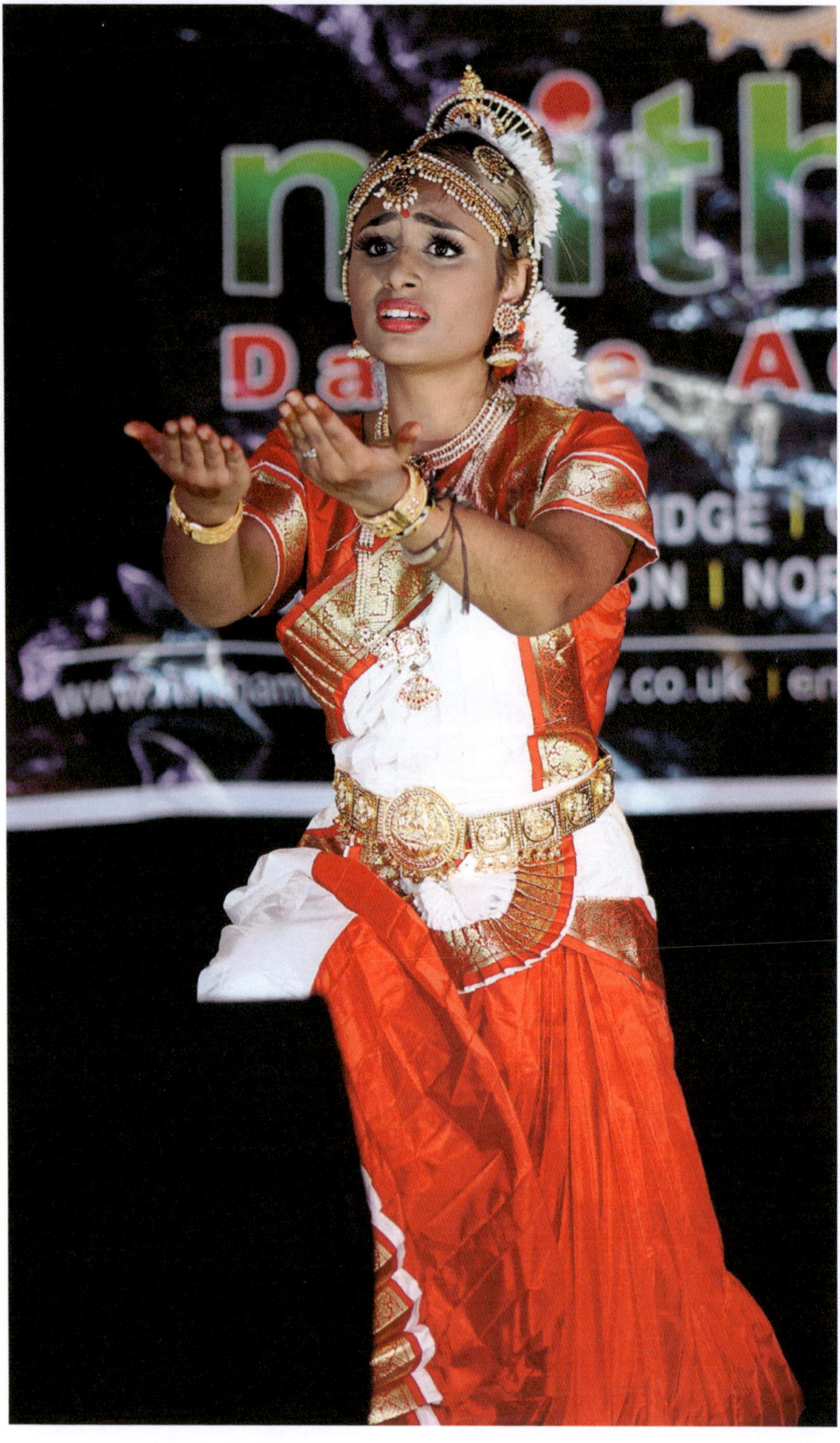

Growing Up and Thriving in Two Very Different Cultures

Growing Up and Thriving in Two Very Different Cultures

Growing Up and Thriving in Two Very Different Cultures

Growing Up and Thriving in Two Very Different Cultures

Growing Up and Thriving in Two Very Different Cultures

Growing Up and Thriving in Two Very Different Cultures

Growing Up and Thriving in Two Very Different Cultures

Growing Up and Thriving in Two Very Different Cultures

Mrs Sujatha Chenilath

7 EPILOGUE

My journey with photography began in the 1960s, and now, more than 60 years later, I've grown from having just a general interest in the subject, to it becoming something way bigger, something which actually defines my life now. Being retired, I now have lots of time to read, to digest and consider what I've read and learned, and to put into play those things that enable me to put out the best photography I have ever done.

This 'Nritham Project' has been in my mind and heart for ten years now, and it finally began in earnest during October of 2021. It was then that I was introduced to something that was consciously new to me, but something that was always around me and accepted as normal by others of Asian descent.

I grew up in, worked in, and initially retired in, a world that consisted mainly of people just like me.

White, Anglo-Saxon, English speaking, Protestants.

I wasn't brought up with, nor did I ever knowingly have, racist thoughts or bias, but then again, how would someone develop those biases if one is not exposed to them in the first place? And when I retired from my working life to the coast of Oregon, living in a small and tight-knit community of 6,800 population, although the location and surroundings were idyllic, everyone 'looked' the same.

White, Anglo-Saxon, English speaking, Protestants.

So imagine what it was like for me to retire (again) to a small village just outside of Bedford in Bedfordshire and become integrated into a world where on any given day, I would hear conversations being conducted in

Growing Up and Thriving in Two Very Different Cultures

Italian, Spanish, French, Swedish, Norwegian, Kurdish, and dozens of others too numerous to name! I found great joy in going to London, taking the underground to the Covent Garden station at noontime, finding a light lunch in a small sidewalk cafe, and while eating, hearing what certainly were one hundred different languages being spoken by passers-by! And everyone was getting along, everyone appeared happy with their lives and themselves! The diversity of people and the different foods and tastes and aromas; these past ten years, this latest part of my life, has been like going back to the classroom, every day. Exciting to me, really, *really* exciting!

But then what really struck me as nothing less than awe-inspiring - when I began my association with Sujatha and her students (ages between 4 and 19) - was the fact that all these young people spoke at least three completely different languages, but additionally they were able to understand and get by with even more languages and dialects! At times during practices, Sujatha would be explaining a dance move, start out in her native language, and mid-sentence change to English! The students didn't miss a beat. At 80 years old, I sometimes have trouble with English! Colour me humbled, to be certain.

The young people I worked with during this project were always polite, always respectful (of me and each other) and always willing to help their friends with learning routines and such. Their parents were always cordial, respectful and inquisitive about how I was doing, and thankful when I would share some of my work with them directly. To be invited into someone's home for a meal - in the Asian culture - is an honour, and that has happened to me while enjoying work on this project.

So now that Vaughan Dean has helped me complete two successful exhibitions and helped create this book you hold in your hands, I can move on to other projects knowing that the people I have worked with over the past 2+ years are, or will be, well prepared for life in the 21st century. They'll be able to feel comfortable communicating with the world, and will be a real asset to humanity.

For sure, this will be in part to their Asian cultural upbringing, but also because Mrs. Sujatha Chenilath was in their lives. My sincere thanks for allowing me to be in all your lives; you've given me far more than I will ever be able to give you.

Warmly,

Cliff

Printed in Great Britain
by Amazon